Dear Friend,

One of the greatest concerns of my father, Dr. D. James Kennedy, was that Christians be armed with the facts of Scripture, history, and science to explain and defend their faith. As it says in 1 Peter 3:15, "... always be ready to give a defense to everyone who asks you a reason for the hope that is in you, with meekness and fear." We are to "be prepared" as the motto of the Boy Scouts says.

The Real Messiah: Prophecies Fulfilled is designed to help you do just that. It is a new revised edition of my father's original book, *Messiah: Prophecies Fulfilled*. Coauthored by Dr. Jerry Newcombe, who colabored with my father on numerous other books, it shows compelling evidence that Jesus was indeed God. In Isaiah 9:6 it says, "For unto us a Child is born, unto us a Son is given; and the government will be upon His shoulder. And His name will be called Wonderful, Counselor, Mighty God, Everlasting Father, Prince of Peace."

As Christians, our faith is not a blind faith. It's marvelous to know our faith is both logical and reasonable but most importantly, that it is the truth. This book presents the prophecies written hundreds of years before Christ's birth and uniquely fulfilled by Him in His birth, life, death, and resurrection. It will instill confidence in your own heart and mind about the claims of Scripture and enable you to defend the faith with confidence, passion, and power.

In Christ,

Jennifer Kennedy Cassidy

Jennifer Kennedy Cassidy

THE REAL
MESSIAH

THE REAL
MESSIAH

PROPHECIES FULFILLED

D. JAMES KENNEDY, Ph.D.
and JERRY NEWCOMBE, D. Min.

the
D. JAMES KENNEDY
FOUNDATION

Published by The D. James Kennedy Foundation

Jacket and Interior Design: Roark Creative, www.roarkcreative.com

Cover image: *The Adoration of the Shepherds,* detail of the group surrounding Jesus (oil on canvas). Museo Nazionale di San Martino, Naples, Italy

ISBN: 9780615227283

Printed in the United States of America

D. James Kennedy Foundation
980 N. Federal Highway, Suite 440
Boca Raton, FL 33432

CONTENTS

FOREWORD

One amazing aspect of the Bible is the fact that it contains scores and scores of prophecies that were written hundreds of years before Jesus was born, and were fulfilled during His lifetime, proving beyond a reasonable doubt that Jesus is the Messiah. Only a sovereign God could look into the future and predict details so accurately.

Several years ago, my dear friend and mentor, the late D. James Kennedy, Ph.D., wrote a short book on the subject, *Messiah: Prophecies Fulfilled*. We believe so strongly in that book that we decided to expand and revise it, including even more prophecies fulfilled. We are calling this update *The Real Messiah: Prophecies Fulfilled*. Note that the Hebrew word "Messiah" is "Christ" in the Greek and means "The Anointed One" in English. Christ is not Jesus' last name; it is His title.

We begin this revised book with a lengthy Christmas meditation that my wife and I have sent out to family and friends. We have received such good feedback on it, and it ties in so well to the topic at hand, that we open this revised and expanded book with what I believe is a fascinating study.

Donald E. Van Curler, Publisher
Christmas 2008

Star of Wonder*

❧

[W]e saw His star in the East and have come to worship Him.
Matthew 2:2

More than 1,800 years before Jesus was born, the book of Job declared: "When the morning stars sang together, and all the sons [angels] of God shouted for joy" (Job 38:7). The stars sang together in celebration of God's creation.

Jumping ahead to the time of Jesus' birth, the "star of wonder" appeared in the sky. As Phillips Brooks worded it in his classic Christmas carol, "O Little Town of Bethlehem:" "O morning stars, together proclaim the holy birth."

Writing more than 700 years before Christ, Isaiah proclaims: "The glory of the LORD shall be revealed, and all flesh shall see it together; for the mouth of the LORD has spoken" (Isaiah 40:5).

"FOR WE HAVE SEEN HIS STAR"

Two thousand years ago, the Christmas star led the wise men to look for their king. It was "*His* star." Matthew writes, "wise men from the East came to Jerusalem" (Matthew 2:1). The magi—the wise men—were overjoyed to see the star. After they went out of Jerusalem, the "star which they had seen in the East went before

*Note: We recognize this is a subject on which even learned scholars do not all agree.

The Wise Men Guided by the Star

them" and "stood over where the young Child was." It is interesting to note that the magi came to see the *child*, not the baby. Certainly, God could have used a supernatural phenomenon to announce the birth of His Son to them, as He did to the shepherds. He could have, but instead, it appears He used a natural event—a simple, ordinary circumstance—to work His awesome will.

He used a star to mark the birth of a King.

The magi saw the first sign in their homeland. Then, along the way they saw a second sign, and soon after that they left Jerusalem and traveled five miles—to Bethlehem—a third appearing. Three? A triune God? Three in one? Remember the first verse in the Bible? Genesis 1:1: "In the beginning God...." In Hebrew, one of the names for God is "Elohim," a plural indicator—a plural word. Three.

The starry gift is from God to man.

"GOD WITH US"

Christmas. Its wonderful message is all about our Lord, Immanuel, which means "God with us." He, Jesus, who resides in Heaven, who is co-eternal and co-equal with the Father and the Holy Spirit, came to our world—breathed our air—knew our pain and died for our sin. He Himself, in human form, came to open the way to His Heaven.

It happened on a most beautiful night—with stars like diamonds sparkling on a black velvet background. It was just another quiet night, and they were simple sheep and ordinary shepherds. God moved in such a simple setting. Presumably, the shepherds were sound asleep. Then came words. They were awakened in an instant. "[A]nd they were greatly afraid" (Luke 2:9). Startled, they opened their eyes to see an angel—an angel who was telling them: "Do not be afraid, for behold, I bring you good tidings of great joy which will be to all people. For there is born to you this day in the city of David a Savior, who is Christ the Lord" (Luke 2:10-11).

Do not be afraid?

Great joy?

A Savior?

Right out of the night. Right there for all to see. The shepherds were shaking.

Today, God lovingly smiles down on us because of that Savior— and because of His only begotten Son's death and resurrection. He came to earth, and He finished the job that was left undone by Adam.[1] That is grace. That is amazing grace. The Bible tells us, "For by grace you have been saved through faith, and that not of yourselves; it is the gift of God, not of works, lest anyone should boast" (Ephesians 2:8-9).

We will return to that historic night in a moment, but first here are some fascinating facts that provide a helpful background. Daybreak races across the face of our world at more than one thousand miles per hour (actually 1,040 miles per hour). The earth moves around the sun at the rate of 66,700 miles per hour, traveling 1,600,800 miles per day. Daybreak lights up mountains and valleys and sweeps away the stars.

Isaac Abrabanel, born in Lisbon in 1437, treasurer of King Ferdinand and Queen Isabella, a financial genius, a Bible scholar, believed in Jesus and wrote four books on Messianic prophecies. He was an astronomer and wrote about Jewish astrologers from a school at Sippar, Babylonia, who were regarded as wise men. He wrote that some ancient astronomers predicted that the Messiah would be born when Jupiter and Saturn were in conjunction with the sign of Pisces, but he did not put together the fact that Jesus' birth had already occurred at such a sign.

In May of the year 7 B.C. (by our calendar), the two largest planets, Jupiter and Saturn (which some call "the wanderer") came within one degree of each other just before daybreak in the eastern sky. On October 5 of that same year, the two came together again—at midnight—directly overhead. Then, for the third time, on December 1, 7 B.C., the planets were once again in conjunction—this time in the southwestern sunset sky.

A conjunction is a close meeting of two planets as they travel in their regular orbits. A triple conjunction occurs once every 805 years, but this time there were some highly significant added features.

Those who studied these signs saw this conjunction occurring in the zodiacal sign of Pisces, the constellation of the Mediterranean Sea. Please note that these astronomical studies existed long before today's astrologers and their New Age followers distorted them, to humanity's detriment. As the late D. James Kennedy pointed out, a strong case can be made that the overall purpose of the signs was to point to the Gospel of Jesus Christ.[2] It's worth noting as well that the Bible names most of these constellations.

To the ancient astronomers, the planet Jupiter was a sign of the coming of a very great king. According to ancient Jewish scholars, Saturn was believed to be the protecting "star" of Israel. Their predictions? A great king had been born to the people of Israel—the King of kings—right in their neighborhood.

Those Babylonian wise men arranged an expedition to observe the events portended in the sky. They started their travels in October and reached Jerusalem in December by traveling about twenty miles each day.

The Star of Bethlehem was no mystery to these wise men. They knew the Scriptures, and they studied the stars. According to a sixteenth century writer: "It was a speciale fierie Ball traveling through the sky above their heads, but not a star." But what was it? A supernova? A comet? A fire ball? Or just a group of planets? None of these compares with the simple description in Matthew 2.

> Now after Jesus was born in Bethlehem of Judea in the days of Herod the king, behold, wise men from the East came to Jerusalem, saying, "Where is He who has been born King of the Jews? For we have seen His star in the East and have come to worship Him."... Then Herod, when he had secretly called the wise men, determined from them what time the star appeared....When they heard the king, they departed; and behold, the star which they had seen in the East went before them, till it came and stood over where the young Child was. When they saw the star, they rejoiced with exceedingly great joy (Matthew 2:1-2, 7, 9-10).

Whatever it was, God used this event to bring wealthy, powerful, highly educated men to meet a little child in Bethlehem—a young boy they knew would be a king. As we will see, this was also foretold by the Hebrew prophets.

In 1989, the late Dr. D. James Kennedy wrote *The Real Meaning of the Zodiac*, detailing the significance of the twelve zodiac signs from a Christian perspective. He noted that Pisces ("fishes") illustrated deliverance out of bondage to the ancients. It told of God's deliverance of people from all nations out of the slavery of sin into the glorious light of His love through the preaching of His Gospel.

> And Jesus, walking by the Sea of Galilee, saw two brothers, Simon called Peter, and Andrew his brother, casting a net into the sea; for they were fishermen. Then He said to them, "Follow Me, and I will make you fishers of men" (Matthew 4:18,19).

These fish are a representation of the Church. Through the Gospel, Christ delivers His people from spiritual bondage, from the bondage of sin.

"THE HEAVENS DECLARE THE GLORY OF THE LORD"

Pisces ("fishes") was actually the symbol of Israel thousands of years ago, and it was also the ancient symbol of the Church. A believer would make a mark in the sand or dirt with an upward curved slash and another would finish the image with a downward sloped slash—completing the symbol of a fish—indicating that he or she, too, was a believer in Jesus. The fish is still a symbol of Christianity; today we see it displayed on the back of cars, for instance.

The Greek word, *Ichthus*, is an acrostic representation of Jesus' name and titles equivalent to the Greek word for "fish." (The direct English translation of this acrostic is: "Jesus Christ, God's Son, Savior.") The Latin word, *Pisces*, also means fish.

In ancient Egypt, this constellation was known as *Pi-Cot Orion*

16

or *Pisces Hori*, which means "The fish of Him who comes" (fishes that belong to that One who is coming—fishes that belong to Christ).

Isn't it fascinating to know that some of the stars in each of these star clusters are also names of fish? The brightest one is *Al Samaca*, which means "The Upheld." In Isaiah 41:10, God says: "I will uphold you with my righteous right hand" (ESV). As the fishes of Christ, we are upheld by His mighty hand.

Another star in this constellation is *Okda*. This is a Hebrew word meaning "The United." These two "fishes," Al Samaca and Okda, could be said to represent all believers—those of the Old Testament, who looked forward to the Christ, and those of the New Testament, who believe in Jesus the Christ. The Old Testament prophesied that the old and the new would be revealed at a future time and be bound together, united. For example, Jeremiah foretells the day that God would make a new covenant (a new testament) with His people (Jeremiah 31:31).

Meanwhile, Jesus said to His disciples, "Come after Me, and I will make you become fishers of men" (Mark 1:17). The Church is likened to fishes encircled in a fisherman's net. We remember the incident in John 21, when the disciples' net was full, holding 153 large fish, yet "the net was not broken." There are many members in the Church today, and there is room for many more.

Christ was talking to fishermen—Peter, Simon, and James—and telling them: "Follow Me, and I will make you fishers of men." This was a commandment ("Follow Me") followed by a promise ("I will make you…"), showing Christ's passion for souls. We know from Romans 10:9 that when we believe (another command), we shall "be saved" (a promise). It is a passion of Christ to save souls. If we are not becoming fishers of men, how can we claim to be followers of Christ? Christ expects each of us to exhibit His passion for lost souls.

These are just a few examples of the hundreds of signs God put before us, neatly arranged in the stars of His heavens so that the world would know and see His glory. He did this long before the Bible was written— "when the morning stars sang together."

RETURNING TO THE STAR

The Bible used the words "gone before" and "stand over" referring to the Christmas star—so it had to be something quite obvious and one that all could recognize—a star that would move slowly across the sky.

In 1603, Johannes Kepler was the Royal Mathematician and Astronomer to the court of Prague when he noticed a conjunction of Saturn and Jupiter in the constellation of Pisces. In 1603 it was expected to be visible in late December and into January of 1604. Because of the timing, Kepler wondered whether another earlier conjunction might have been that of the prophesied Star of Bethlehem.

He studied his charts and noticed that the event happened every 805 years. The two occurrences would have been 1610 years apart— and subtracting the date 1604 would indicate that the year 6 B.C. should have been the correct date. Then Kepler remembered that the Jewish rabbi Isaac Abrabanel had written that the prophesied Messiah would be born in one of these signs. However, the "six years" bothered him, and he did not pursue the matter further.

In the early 1900s, archaeologists found, north of Babylon, the legendary ancient Sippar (now in Iraq) and its vast store of thousands of cuneiform tablets describing the motion of the stars for each day, for centuries.

In 1926, Herr Schnabel, a German professor, translated those tablets and came across the record of the conjunction of Jupiter and Saturn converging four times in 7 B.C. and six times in 6 B.C. He remembered Kepler's notes. He also knew that Dionysius Exiguus' original calculations were wrong by about six years. (Around 525 A.D., a monk, named Dionysius Exiguus created the Christian calendar, B.C. and A.D., but he was off in his calculations by a few years. So, ironically, Christ was actually born "Before Christ.")

THE MAGI

Back to the wise men who came from the East. Who were they, exactly? They were "magi," a word that comes from the old Persian word, *magu*. The Greek historian, Herodotus, first mentioned these magi as a tribe of Medes with priestly functions. Later, the term wise men applied to astrologers. Epiphany (January 6) is a celebration which marks the visit of the magi to worship Jesus.

Persian Muslims invaded Bethlehem in the seventh century, and they destroyed church after church. However, they spared the Church of the Nativity because of its beautiful mosaic depiction of the wise men—wearing Persian clothes.

The Bible does not tell us the number of the wise men, but the real number of them, with servants, must have been twelve or more. Matthew writes that these wise men from the East had seen an unusual star that they had identified with the newborn "King of the Jews." They called it "His star." This king was so important in their minds that they planned a long journey to find Him. These were men of great wealth, and they were transporting valuable gifts, so armed guards would have been necessary.

They made up a caravan which followed the Euphrates, turning southwest along the Fertile Crescent. The ancient trade routes they traveled made their journey more than a thousand miles from point to point. The straight-line distance is about 500 miles, but few would have risked traveling an empty desert route with no roads.

Upon their arrival in Jerusalem, they would have found many other traders' caravans, since the city was on the busy trade route between Europe, Africa, and Asia.

There the wise men would have asked the locals about the great King (Jupiter) who was to have been born to the Jews (Saturn) in this land of Judea (Pisces).

Again, in Matthew 2:1-3, we read:

> Now after Jesus was born in Bethlehem of Judea
> in the days of Herod the king, behold, wise men

19

from the East came to Jerusalem, saying, "Where is
He who has been born King of the Jews? For we
have seen His star in the East and have come to worship Him."

Can you picture that day in the city? We know from the Bible
and the ancient historian Josephus that the political leader, Herod,
was a murderous old man who was continually fearful that someone
would take his power and his throne from him.

We can just imagine his reaction when he heard the question.
He talked to the religious leaders and inquired of them about Scriptures that prophesied a Messiah and His birth. The Hebrew prophet
Micah, writing about 750 years before Jesus' birth, stated: "But you,
Bethlehem Ephrathah, though you are little among the thousands
of Judah, yet out of you shall come forth to Me the One to be Ruler
in Israel" (Micah 5:2).

Bethlehem?

Why had no one ever told Herod? The star they were talking
about was not so obvious to Herod or anyone else in Jerusalem. People he talked with knew little about any star. Herod told them about
the child that was supposed to have been born in Bethlehem—just
five miles away. No one seemed to know about it.

So Herod asked the wise men, "When you have found Him,
bring back word to me, that I may come and worship Him also"
(Matthew 2:8).

Perhaps the wise men knew all about Herod and his wicked reputation. He worshiped no God—only himself. I am of the opinion
that the magi did not trust him. Furthermore, God explicitly warned
them not to return to Herod, so they avoided him.

After meeting Herod, the wise men and their helpers likely left
by the south gate of Jerusalem and traveled the long, winding valley
to Bethlehem watching the sunset all the while.

Suddenly, in the glow of the sunset, right over the little town
ahead, they saw the evening star, and not only did they see their

third conjunction—their goal—but Saturn and Jupiter had been joined by Mars in a blazing triangle of light. Three in one. Three again.

> When they heard the king, they departed; and behold, the star which they had seen in the East went before them, till it came and stood over where the young Child was. When they saw the star, they rejoiced with exceedingly great joy (Matthew 2:9,10).

His star was that light. Jupiter, the king star they were watching, as the other two planets moved close, had signaled the birth of the *king*.

Actually a better translation would be: "The star that they had seen ... had gone before them." So now we know that the star they were watching was not a moving light. Remember Balaam's fourth prophecy of Israel to Balak? "I see Him, but not now; I behold Him, but not near; a Star shall come out of Jacob..." (Numbers 24:17). Moses wrote that about 1700 B.C. in the plains of Moab by Jordan near Jericho, just before the entrance into Canaan. Here was the Star coming out of Bethlehem.

The wise men found the little rented house. The star stood right over it. The word used for "the Child" in Matthew 2 is not the same word used in the earlier account when the shepherds came the night of Jesus' birth. Earlier, it was the "newly born" (*brephos*) that the angels told the startled shepherds about. Now, for the wise men, it is "the little boy" (*paidion*). He was no longer just a baby, but rather, a little boy.

"And when they had come into the house, they saw the young Child with Mary His mother, and fell down and worshiped Him..." (Matthew 2:11). The magi brought gifts of gold to represent Jesus as king, frankincense to represent God, and myrrh to represent Him as Savior.

They knew they had found the Savior, the precious Son of Almighty God, the King of Kings—Our Lord and Savior Jesus Christ.

Presumably, the wise men retired early at the inn. By this time, there would have been plenty of room for them. But a few hours later, God warned them in a dream, and at midnight they awoke. They left quickly and quietly, avoiding Jerusalem, most likely traveling on the coastal road—then across Galilee to the King's Highway, and headed back to their homes.

They believed. They saw Him. They had to tell the world.

We who know Him must go and do likewise.

PART ONE

Christmas According
to the Prophets

INTRODUCTION

Who is the real Messiah? Who will save us? Who will come charging on a white horse to vanquish all evil? Who will make all things right with the world? Who will bring true peace to the world? As the psalmist put it, "Who is the King of Glory? The Lord Almighty He is the King of Glory" (Psalm 24:10). Jesus is the answer to these questions.

Jesus Christ is the most important human being who ever lived. In Him is our hope and our destiny. All of humanity will one day have to stand before Him because He has been entrusted with the role of humanity's Judge. Jesus is the key to understanding the Old Testament. He is the key to understanding the New Testament. He is the key to understanding history. In fact, He is the key to understanding the meaning of life.

Still, most people do not realize the extent to which Jesus Christ is spoken of in the Old Testament, which is sometimes called the Hebrew Bible. To examine much of that evidence is the purpose of this volume.

You could formulate an outline of the life of Jesus Christ just by studying the Old Testament. Now that we know the entirety of Jesus' life, we can see its overall direction in the Old Testament, if we just look for it.

In his recent, best-selling atheistic screed, *Letter to a Christian Nation*, author Sam Harris dismisses the prophecies about Jesus as unimportant. He essentially ignores them. Instead, he criticizes the Bible, saying that if there were a God, and if this were really His Word, then He should have revealed mathematical formulas or scientific principles in it. Instead of humanity slowly learning such things over the centuries, God—according to Harris—should have revealed to ancient man information that only modern man can comprehend. Our response to this, to paraphrase what God said to

Job, is: Where was Sam Harris when the Lord created the heavens and the earth? The Bible is a spiritual book. It deals with eternal issues. It is for all people and all places and all times and contains all we need for life and godliness. Sam Harris, and others like him, claim to know better than God what should or should not be in His Word, while ignoring the divine nature of what is revealed.

This reminds me of charges that some critics of the Bible levy against the book. For example, the Bible refers to sunrise and sunset, even though we know the sun stands still and the earth moves, so the sun does not really rise and set. But modern communicators also refer to the sunrise and sunset. What Harris and other critics miss is simply this: That all the Old Testament prophecies point to God's plan and purpose for humanity. The single most important message of the Bible (Old and New Testaments) is the death of our Lord on behalf of sinners. This is the heart and soul of the prophecies. Meanwhile, the Apostle Paul says this about the skeptics and the Cross: "For the message of the cross is foolishness to those who are perishing, but to us who are being saved it is the power of God" (1 Corinthians 1:18).

There is a unity in the Bible's overall message, and the sacrifice of Jesus for our sins is the heart and soul of God's redemptive plan:

1) God made us and loves us.
2) But all of humanity sins and that sin separates us from God.
3) God is holy and must punish sin.
4) Without the shedding of blood, there is no forgiveness of sins.
5) The blood of sheep and goats temporarily satisfied this need for sacrifice, while pointing to the true fulfillment of all these sacrifices, which took place when Jesus died for sinners.
6) We must believe in Him and repent from our sins.

Everything else in the Bible is a variation of these principles, including how we should live in light of them.

Hundreds of years before the miraculous baby was born in Bethlehem, and changed the whole world, His coming was foretold. The purpose of Part I of this book is to provide an overview of the subject, beginning with the wondrous story of Christmas and how that, too, was foretold. In this first section, we will also consider the staggering odds against Jesus fulfilling these prophecies and respond to skeptics who do not accept them.

C. S. Lewis described conditions in the world without Christ as: "always winter, but never Christmas." Christmas is so uplifting to the soul. Long before the baby was born, long before the shepherds worshiped, long before the wise men came, the Hebrew prophets spoke of this great hope.

CHAPTER 1

The Joy of Christmas

❧

Do not be afraid, for behold,
I bring you good tidings of great joy.
Luke 2:10

Thousands of years before He was born, the coming of Jesus of Nazareth was foretold. When He finally came, He fulfilled hundreds of prophecies.

Even secular writers who have dared to look at the life of Jesus and some of the prophecies about Him—His birth, His life, His death—have conceded that it is an "unsolved mystery." To the believer, this "unsolved mystery" points to the miraculous intervention of God, who knows the end and the beginning and who pointed the way for His Messiah. Again, Christ is not Jesus' last name; it is His title. He is *the* Messiah, the Anointed One, the only mediator between God and man. The purpose of this book is to show that the life of Jesus was miraculously foretold. The more details we learn about Jesus, the more clearly we see that He is God's Messiah.

When Jesus came to Earth the first time, He was not recognized for who He really was. One of the most amazing facts of all is that the ones who rejected Him actually *fulfilled prophecy* in the process of rejecting Him. Their hatred of Jesus consumed and blinded them to the irony of what they were doing. Thus, they became unwitting players in a drama foretold hundreds of years before. Rabbi Moshe Laurie, a Messianic rabbi from Connecticut, remarks:

> [M]ost people that ask me, "Well, why was the Messiah denied?" Because, you see, if He [were] not denied, He would've not fulfilled His prophecy. And He would not be the Messiah.[3]

The apostle Paul actually made a very similar remark in a synagogue. He said of Jesus and His mistreatment by the temple authorities: "For those who dwell in Jerusalem, and their rulers, because they did not know Him, nor even the voices of the Prophets which are read every Sabbath, have fulfilled them [the prophecies] in condemning Him" (Acts 13:27).

But long before Good Friday, there was Christmas.

THE MAJESTY OF CHRISTMAS

Christmas weaves its own magic spell, with twinkling lights and silver bells transforming the landscape into a winter wonderland. Christmas waves its magic wand and, behold, everything is lovelier and softer and more beautiful than before. Christmas works its annual enchantment and carols float on the air and sing in the heart. "Bah, humbug!" is changed into "Merry Christmas." There is a surge of love and kindness not felt at any other time of the year.

Christmas *is* the most wonderful time of the year. A starlit night, a crude shelter, a lantern swinging from a beam, cattle chewing their cud, shepherds standing at the door, a travel-weary young woman, a simple village carpenter, the song of angels, and a babe lying in a manger. These are the simple parts of that artless and lovely story for which children never lose their delight and age never loses its affection.

What a difference that day has made! The story of the birth brings the prodigal home; it softens the blows of adversity; it takes the sting out of defeat; it puts a song in the heart; it gives new meaning and purpose to life. Yes, Christmas is the most wonderful time of the year.

IT WAS ALL FORETOLD

Long before the first Christmas, the ancient Hebrew prophets foretold it. They told about One coming who would be born in Bethlehem. He would be of the line of David (and thus, of Abraham's, Isaac's, Jacob's, and Judah's line). He would be worshiped by foreign rulers who would come from the East. He would be a Son who was born as a human, and yet He would be God.

As we will see later, the Old Testament foretold:

- Who His ancestors would be, including Abraham, Isaac, Jacob, Judah, Jesse, and David;
- That He would be born of a virgin;
- That His name would be called Immanuel (meaning God with us);
- That He would be born in Bethlehem (a small village); and
- That He would live for a while in Egypt.

Christmas is an annual source of joy, and to think it was foretold long before it took place adds an extra element of wonder. This book will explore numerous details of the life of Jesus Christ, revealing that the Hebrew prophet, Isaiah, could just as well be called a Gospel writer. In fact, Part III of this book is called "The Gospel According to Isaiah."

HIS BIRTH

After His ancient lineage, we look at His birth. The very first of the biblical prophecies is that He would be born of the seed of a woman. Throughout all Scripture no one else but the Messiah is ever called the "seed of a woman." The reference is always to the seed of a man. In general, women are not even mentioned in biblical genealogies.[4] But here is a virgin who is going to conceive, and here is the One who is to be the seed only of a woman—a difficult thing to arrange, especially before one is conceived.

How could someone prearrange his own birth? He would have to be born in Bethlehem, and He would have to make sure, also, that His goings forth have been from of old, even from everlasting which, of course, reminds us of the fact that He is God, and could therefore arrange all such things, because the prophet Isaiah said, almost 750 years before He was born:

> For unto us a Child is born, unto us a Son is given; and the government will be upon His shoulder. And His name will be called Wonderful, Counselor, Mighty God, Everlasting Father, Prince of Peace (Isaiah 9:6).

And so it was that this One who came forth in the tiny town of Bethlehem, on the particular day prophesied by Daniel, had been going on forever.

THE PERSISTENCE OF CHRISTMAS

Perhaps, the most amazing thing about Christmas is its persistence. Age cannot affect it; time does not efface it; the centuries have not dimmed its glory. At each recurring yuletide, our reverence for it increases, and our fascination with it intensifies.

In the darkest hours of life, men have found in it their peace. In deepest desperation, men have found in it their consolation. In death's cold embrace, they have found in it their hope. Just when you think the world is through with it, it meets you coming around the corner. Somehow, in the midst of all the rough and tumble of history, it has elbowed its way down to the present. The swirl of hatred cannot bury it. The oceans of misunderstanding cannot drown it. The avalanche of distortion cannot hide it, and all the armies of the world have been unable to destroy it. Christmas abides, and it brings with it the most joyful time of the year.

The keynote of the Christmas story is joy—"We bring you glad

The Nativity of Christ

tidings of great joy." There has been a tragic tendency in the past on the part of many toward "drone religion," "whine religion," "cant religion," "moan religion," "croak religion," or "sepulcher religion." We ought to celebrate religion. Christianity should be exultation, jubilation, exhilaration. Christmas is a triumph and a time for singing. Our worship resounds with hymnody. It sparkles with anthems. It overflows with thanksgiving and praise. It is a time of joy—as the carol proclaims, "Joy to the world, the Lord is come." Arguably the best music in the world belongs to Christmas, such as the rich Christmas carols or Handel's *Messiah* (although originally it was viewed as an Easter oratorio).

In reading Luke 2:10 in the Greek text, it struck me how powerful that phrase is. "*Ephobethason phobon megan,*" which means: "They feared a great fear." They were overwhelmed with terror. I wonder what the effect would be upon some of our modern sophisticated secularists today if, suddenly and unexpectedly, the Divine were to break in upon the human, the eternal were to burst in upon the temporal, and the heavenly were suddenly to be opened up to the earthly. I think that in many cases these sophisticates would find that their false teeth would fall right to the ground and their knees would begin to knock like castanets. Their worst fears would come upon them and they would discover that, alas, there is a God. It is only unbelief that paints God in gloomy colors.

God is the God of all joy, and His first word to us was, "Fear not. Be of good cheer." Even though Scripture says the time will come when men's hearts will fail them for fear, the admonitions repeatedly come: "Be not afraid. Fear not. Let not your hearts be troubled. Be anxious for nothing." For the sovereign and gracious God has come into the midst of all our anxieties and fears and has said that "all will be well." Someone once said that the phrase or idea of "fear not" appears 365 times in Scripture. I have never counted to verify that, but it is a pleasant thought. Let the corners of lips turn up, for Christ is born in Bethlehem as the ancient prophet Micah predicted and joy has come to the world.

The great Charles Spurgeon said that it is not just joy we are to have, but great joy, good tidings of great joy. He said:

> Man is like a harp, unstrung, and the music of his soul's living strings is discordant, his whole nature wails with sorrow; but the Son of David, that mighty harpist, has come to restore the harmony of humanity, and where His gracious fingers move among the strings, the touch of the fingers of an incarnate God brings forth music as sweet as that of the spheres, and melody as rich as a seraph's canticle.

Though earth's joys often are few, Heaven has poured out an

ocean of joy on the parched souls of men.

GREAT JOY

Good tidings of great joy. That is what the Christian religion is all about. "For unto you is born this day in the City of David a Savior." He is born. We are not merely talking about an idea, a philosophy, a theological dictum or doctrine or dogma. We are talking about a fact, an historic event, a concrete happening. It was predicted. It came to be. Jesus Christ was born in Bethlehem. He lived and He suffered under Pontius Pilate, and with those words, the life of Jesus Christ is pounded into the bedrock of history. He died and rose again the third day.

Unlike all other religions, which are nothing more than religio-philosophies, Christianity is based upon facts and upon evidence, evidence which is absolutely incontrovertible. In spite of all criticism, in spite of all charges of infidelity, those facts remain as untouched and undisturbed as when they first occurred in this world. Christ was born "this day" said the angel. "This day" in history; "this day" exactly as predicted by the prophet Daniel in the very year that He was to come. (For more detail, please see Chapter 17.)

He came, we are told, "in the fullness of time." Just at the time when the world was most desperately in need of a Savior, He came. When the golden age of Greek philosophy was past and an intellectual barrenness covered the landscape of the mind, when faith in the Homeric gods had all but vanished completely and skepticism palled the souls of men, when the moral structures of society had collapsed everywhere and man had sunk deep into the mire of depravity and vice, then. Then. Then Jesus Christ came into the world. In the fullness of time. Exactly at the moment He was most needed.

Philip Schaff, the great nineteenth-century historian, says that the history of mankind before that day must be viewed as a preparation for His coming and that all of the history after His birth is the diffusion of His spirit and the progress of His kingdom in this world. Jesus Christ split the ages in half, as with a divine scimitar.

Such is the power of that single life, born into the world on that glorious day.

This life not only confounded all the sophistry of the scribes and Pharisees and silenced the subtleties of the Sadducees; it not only demonstrated the futility and the fallacy of Greek philosophy, but also caused the very throne of Caesar to tremble. At last, it finally brought the entire structure of pagan heathenism crashing down into the dust. All this was accomplished by that babe born in Bethlehem.

He grew to manhood and with one hand smote the legalism of Israel. With the other He dealt a death blow to the superstitious ignorance of Gentile paganism. He has continued to trod across the centuries conquering—and is still to conquer. He lifts the ages out of their streams and, taking the gates of death, He rises to the hill of Calvary and casts them into oblivion. There has never been anyone remotely comparable to Jesus of Nazareth, the babe born in Bethlehem. He is the mighty Savior and God.

Yet it seems that in spite of the centuries which have passed and the repetition of the message, there are still many who do not seem to get the point. I think of the story Paul Harvey told some years ago on one of his radio broadcasts. It was about a rather disreputable looking man who appeared at the front door of a beautiful home and asked the lady of the house if there was not some work he could do around the place to earn enough money for a meal. She said to him, "Well, the porch out back could stand painting. There's a can of green paint in the garage." A couple of hours later he reappeared at the door, besprinkled with green paint, and announced that the job was completed. "But, lady," he said, "that's not a Porsche out there, that's a Ferrari." Some people just never get the point.

I talk to people who think they have accepted Jesus Christ as Savior, and all they have done is accept Him as a teacher. Others who think they have accepted Him as Savior have simply accepted Him as their example. Still others have accepted Him as a guide or helper, but Jesus came to do much more than that. He came to be the Savior of the world. He came to save our souls. Nothing less than that will suffice.

THE PURPOSE OF THE SHEEP

Jesus was born in Bethlehem, and it was over the sloping hills outside of Bethlehem that the shepherds were watching their flocks by night. I have visited the site and meditated upon the events of this night, as have many of you.

Do you know why those sheep were being raised? They were being fattened for transport to Jerusalem to be slaughtered on the altars of the temple. It was here amidst those shepherds and their sheep that the announcement came that the Lamb of God was born. The Lamb of God, "who takes away the sin of the world." There would be no more need for lamb or oxen to die. It was the last, the final evening sacrifice. It was our guilt that was to be laid upon Him. He was to have imputed unto Him the sin of the world and there, upon the altar of Calvary, the Lamb of God was to be slain that we might know eternal life. All the Old Testament prescriptions about the sacrifices point to the once and for all sacrifice of Jesus on the Cross.

Dr. Donald Grey Barnhouse was my spiritual father. Someone once gave me a Christmas card that he sent out in 1956, the very year I set out for seminary. The Christmas card contained within it this beautiful poem:

> Not all the blood of beasts on Jewish altars lain
> Could give the guilty conscience peace or wash away the stain.
> But Christ, the Heavenly Lamb, takes all our sins away
> The sacrifice of nobler name and richer blood than they.
> On Christmas Day, God's Lamb was born that He might die.

At crucifixion time He died that we might live on
high.
Thus, life and death in Him were joined in mystery.
His life brought death, His death brought life to us
eternally.[5]

The river of life splits at last into two different streams that flow
in diametrically opposite directions. There are two eternities, the
one as swift, as long, and as mighty as the other. One empties into
an ocean of gladness, opaline above and coralline beneath, and the
other plunges over a cataract of despair, into an abyss of hopeless-
ness. Upon the one there sail argosies of light; upon the other are
found the hulks of the wrecks of lives dismantled by the fiery cy-
clone of divine wrath.

CONCLUSION

"Joy to the world, The Lord is come." What a glorious thought
that is—and joy is precisely what Christmas brings. In fact, one
national survey showed that 90 percent of people in America say
they are happier at Christmastime than at any other time of the
year. The very idea of Christmas paired with sorrow is almost
oxymoronic; the two just do not go together. Christmas and joy go
hand in hand, and joy was born on Christmas morning. And to think,
hundreds of years before the first Christmas, it was all foretold.

CHAPTER 2

Prophets and Profits

❦

Beware of false prophets, who come to you in sheep's clothing,
but inwardly they are ravenous wolves.
Matthew 7:15

Through the years, the nation's leading psychics have made all sorts of outrageous claims, none of which, to my knowledge, have ever come true. A few such predictions:

- "Next year there is going to be a great earthquake that is going to turn Florida into an island;"
- Whoopi Goldberg is going to leave acting and join a convent.
- There is going to be a national lottery, and it is going to cut our taxes in half.
- The "Japanese will discover a cure for the common cold—using a chemical found in the ink spewed out by squid." This idea is not nearly as ludicrous as some of the ink spewed out by psychics, I might mention.
- Major league baseball would have a shot in the arm as they would acquire, "this year," their first female big league baseball player. (This was predicted in the mid-1990s.)
- A pet food company "will discover that a by-product

of its dog-biscuit-making process cures baldness. And this rub-on chemical will become an instant sensation, making millions of baldies happy and hairy again."
- Arnold Schwarzenegger and Roseanne Barr will star in a remake of *Gone With the Wind*.

And on and on it goes.

PROPHECIES UNFULFILLED

Gene Emery, a columnist who covers science and technology, has for years made it part of his duty to examine these would-be "tabloid prophets or psychics" and found that not one of the approximately 100 predictions for a recent year came to pass. He has been keeping track of these "wanna be" prophets since 1978 and says they may be a "hoot to read," but they consistently flop when they try to tell the future.

Still, there are people today spending billions to hear what so-called seers have to say. Do you know who phone psychics are? They are often people hired off the street; yesterday they were truck drivers, ditch diggers, dishwashers, or who knows what. They are given a couple of hours of training in "cold reading," which enables them to pick up on hints you give and then tell you something—enough to satisfy the silly or those who are desperate for some guidance (who are looking in all the wrong places). Tragically, these days we seem to be overrun by a great interest in the occult.

In contrast to all this, one of the most remarkable things in all of the world is the huge number of prophecies that exist in the Old Testament describing a Person who is to come some time in the future, who is to be the Messiah—the Messiah of the Jews and of the whole world. There is nothing in any other sacred or secular writing that even faintly resembles this.

I remember one time I mentioned something about this to a young lady and she said, "Oh prophecies. I'm not much impressed with prophecies. After all," she said, "we have lots of modern prophets today."

I said, "Oh, we do?"

She said, "Yes."

I proceeded to tell her how the modern "prophecies" seem to always get it wrong; whereas, the biblical prophecies always got it right.

Many years ago, my wife bought one of these grocery store celebrity-hype newspapers in January. She kept it for a year and then brought it out and gave it to me saying, "You will find this interesting, I think."

In that edition, there were 61 prophecies by the "ten leading seers in America," and of those 61—again they scored zero. It is truly astonishing that out of 61 prophecies, none of them came to pass.

But what about astrologer Jean Dixon—did she not prophesy that President John F. Kennedy would go to Texas and get shot? No. She did not. She prophesied that somebody who was the person who was going to win the election would be killed. But she also prophesied that the other person was going to win the election. In fact, in one decade, she missed all of the nominees for each of the parties in three elections and all of the presidential winners, as well.

Writer John Lofton states that Jean Dixon predicted that World War III was going to break out in 1958. Maybe you missed that, too. Perhaps you were on vacation. We want to keep you up to date with what's happening in our world. She also predicted that Fidel Castro would be out of power in 1969, and that the Soviets would beat us to the moon, but I do not believe they were waiting for us when we arrived. When you are making this number of predictions, a few of your guesses seem bound to be right—or close to it.

Our modern "prophets" are a joke, or worse. There is a world of difference between the ancient Hebrew prophets, such as Ezekiel, who foretold future events, and today's modern "prophets," many of whom are just out for profits.

Nostradamus is a big hero to many non-Christians today because of his supposedly amazing prophecies such as the rise of one "hister," which fans claim is his prophecy of Hitler. Some even claim

Ezekiel, the Prophet

that Nostradamus allegedly predicted 9/11. The website, www.truthorfiction.com, has proven that this is not true.[6] The accuracy of Nostradamus' prophecies is like a birthday candle compared to the noonday sun of God's amazing prophecies that were fulfilled in Christ.

42

PROPHETS AND PROFITS

I remember the words of a great Christian minister of the last half of the nineteenth century, Charles Haddon Spurgeon, who said he had no doubt that prophesyings are profitable, but he doubted they are as profitable for the hearers and the readers as they are for the writers and the publishers. If he had lived in our day, he would surely have added, "and the 900 number subscribers to the psychic hotlines, as well."

So our modern prophets do not do so well.

TO REPLICATE JUST FOUR PROPHECIES

Stop to think of the difficulty of making accurate prophecies. For example, to prophesy things that are going to happen centuries to come with the kind of accuracy and specificity that exists in Old Testament prophecies boggles the mind. These are not vague generalities; they are incredibly specific. To successfully replicate these kinds of prophecies, you would have to do something like the following. If you were to sit down today and predict who would be inaugurated president in the year 2700 in the United States, assuming that there will be a United States in 2700, then

- Your prediction must detail where this person will be born, and it must be a small town in a state like Nebraska—a town so small that it's not currently listed on state maps.
- Third, you must describe the various occupations of this president—that he will be a world-renowned teacher, that he will be ordained as a priest, and then that he will become president.
- Then you must predict that he will be accused of treason and executed in a manner of execution which will not be invented for several hundred years.

Would that be difficult? Those are but four prophecies. The Old Testament contains 333 prophecies concerning the coming of Christ which include 456 specific facts or details concerning the Messiah

43

that is to come. Four hundred and fifty-six specific details concerning the life of the Messiah. And all of these were written between 1400 and 400 B.C.—you can see the incredible difficulty that exists.

Bible commentator Dr. Walter Elwell writes:

> Among orthodox rabbis there has never been a lack of conjecture respecting the details of the Messiah's ministry. At one time the rabbis applied no less than 456 passages of Scripture to his person and salvation. … The nature of Messianic prophecy is progressive; each prophecy casts more light on the subject. This occurs, for example, respecting the concept of "seed": Messiah is to be born of a woman (Genesis 3:15), through the line of Shem (9:26) and specifically through Abraham (22:18).[7]

CONCLUSION

There is a lot of gullibility out there. And yet, my friends, there is such a thing as genuine prophecy—but it is *not* obtained from "certified psychics." God did ordain prophets. Unlike any of the other 26 books in the world that claim to be scriptures and are held as such by certain religions, the Bible alone contains specific, predictive, fulfilled prophecies. In fact, it is awash in them.

There are over 2,000 prophecies in the Old Testament alone that have already been fulfilled, again, slightly more than 300 of which deal with the Messiah. The other prophecies deal with all of the major cities of that era and all of the countries that were contiguous or within 1,000 miles of Israel. Their futures are described for us in the Old Testament prophecies, and the consequent fulfillment to these cities and nations fill history books. They can be examined by any high school student with an encyclopedia. There is nothing like this anywhere else in all the world.

CHAPTER 3

Astonishing Prophecies

[W]hen the fullness of the time had come,
God sent forth His Son…
Galatians 4:4

As we have seen, Jesus appears repeatedly in the Old Testament. One could even argue that there are far more than 333 prophecies about Him. Knox Theological Seminary's Dr. Warren Gage contends that in a typological sense there are far more than just 300 prophecies. For example, Jesus Himself likened His crucifixion to the bronze serpent being lifted up in the wilderness (John 3:14; also see Numbers 21:8-9). The early Church Fathers employed this form of typology quite a bit. When we apply a typological mode of interpretation, suddenly we see Jesus on virtually every page of the Old Testament. For the purposes of this book, however, we will focus primarily on the more conventional understanding of prophecy.

THE BIBLE'S FULFILLED PROPHECIES

What is prophecy? Prophecy is defined by the late Adrian Rogers as "pre-written history."[8]

What evidence do we have that the Bible is inspired or God-breathed? First of all, in Deuteronomy 18:22, God tells us how we may know if a prophet is sent from Him: "[W]hen a prophet speaks in the name of the LORD, if the thing does not happen or come to pass, that is the thing which the LORD has not spoken; the prophet has spoken it presumptuously; you shall not be afraid of him."

God alone can prophesy the future. As He looked into the future, He told the ancient Hebrews about One that He would send. Here are some of the prophecies Jesus fulfilled. We will be looking at many of these in greater depth in Parts II and III of this book. Listed after each is the Old Testament reference, along with an approximate year of that particular book of the Bible:

- He would come from the line of Abraham (Genesis 12:3, c. 1400 B.C., cf., Galatians 3:8).
- He would come from the line of Judah, of the line of Isaac and that of Jacob (Genesis 49:10, c. 1400 B.C.).
- He would be from the house of David (Jeremiah 23:5, c. 600 B.C.).
- He would be born of a virgin (Isaiah 7:14, c. 750 B.C.).
- He would be given the throne of David (Psalm 132:11, c. 1000 B.C.).
- This throne would be an everlasting throne (Psalm 45:6, c. 1000 B.C.).
- His name would be called Immanuel (Isaiah 7:14, c. 750 B.C.).
- He would have a forerunner who would proclaim His coming (Malachi 3:1, c. 425 B.C.).
- He would be born in Bethlehem—and not merely any Bethlehem, because there were, in fact, two. He would be born in Bethlehem Ephrathah, which was the small Bethlehem down south in Judea (Micah 5:2, c. 720 B.C.). There was a Bethlehem Zebulun in the northern extreme of Israel.
- He would live for a while in Egypt (Hosea 11:1, c. 700 B.C.).
- His birthplace, Bethlehem, would suffer a massacre of infants (as Herod slaughtered the infants when he heard

of the birth of Jesus) (Jeremiah 31:15, c. 600 B.C.).

- He would be called a Nazarene (Judges 13:5, c. 1040 B.C.).
- He would be zealous for His Father's house (Psalm 69:9, c. 1000 B.C.).
- He would be filled with God's Spirit (Isaiah 61:1, c. 750 B.C.).
- He would miraculously heal many (Isaiah 35:5-6, c. 750 B.C.).
- The blind would see (Isaiah 35:5, c. 750 B.C.).
- The deaf would hear (Isaiah 35:5, c. 750 B.C.).
- The lame would walk (Isaiah 35:6, c. 750 B.C.).
- He would draw the Gentiles to Himself (Isaiah 42:6, c. 750 B.C.).
- He would speak in parables (Psalm 78:2-4, c. 1000 B.C.).
- He would be rejected by His own family and friends (Isaiah 53:3, c. 750 B.C.).
- He would make a triumphal entry into Jerusalem on the foal of a donkey (Zechariah 9:9, c. 500 B.C.).
- He would be praised by little children (Psalm 8:2, c. 1000 B.C.).
- He would not be believed (Isaiah 53:1, c. 750 B.C.).
- A friend would betray Him (Psalm 41:9, c. 1000 B.C.) for a specific amount of money—30 pieces of silver (Zechariah 11:12, c. 500 B.C.).
- He would be anointed with the oil of gladness and the Holy Spirit (Psalm 45:7, c. 1000 B.C.).
- He would be a prophet like unto Moses (Deuteronomy 18:15, c. 1400 B.C.).
- He would proclaim the acceptable year of the Lord, and He would bind up the broken-hearted and proclaim liberty to the captive (Isaiah 61:1, c. 700 B.C.).
- He would grow up in humility, poverty, and meekness with a lack of ostentation and a fullness of compassion

and tenderness (Isaiah 42:2, c. 700 B.C.).
- He would be a man of sorrows, acquainted with grief (Isaiah 53:3, c. 750 B.C.).
- He would be forsaken by all of His followers (Zechariah 13:7, c. 500 B.C.).
- He would be scourged and spat upon (Isaiah 50:6, c. 750 B.C.).
- His bounty would be used to buy a potter's field (Zechariah 11:12, c. 500 B.C.).
- He would be given gall and vinegar to drink (Psalm 69:21, c. 1000 B.C.).
- He would suffer the piercing of His hands and feet (Psalm 22:16, c. 1000 B.C.).
- His garments would be divided among His crucifiers, who would gamble for them (Psalm 22:18, c. 1000 B.C.).
- He would be surrounded and ridiculed by His enemies (Psalm 22:12-13, 16-17, c. 1000 B.C.).
- He would thirst (Psalm 22:15, c. 1000 B.C.).
- He would commend His spirit to God the Father (Psalm 31:5, c. 1000 B.C.).
- Not a bone of His body would be broken (Exodus 12:46, c. 1400 B.C.).
- He would be buried with the rich (Isaiah 53:9, c. 750 B.C.).
- He would be raised from the dead (Psalm 16:10, c. 1000 B.C.).
- He would ascend to heaven (Psalm 68:18, c. 1000 B.C.).
- He would become a high priest greater than Aaron—in the order of Melchizedek (Psalm 110:4, c. 1000 B.C.).
- He would be seated at God's right hand (Psalm 110:1, c. 1000 B.C.).
- He would become a smiting scepter (Psalm 2:9, c. 1000 B.C.).
- He would rule the Gentiles (Psalm 2:8, c. 1000 B.C.).

The Brazen Serpent

- He would work wondrous miracles, such as the blind having their eyes opened, the ears of the deaf being unstopped, the lame leaping, and the dumb singing (Isaiah 35:5-6, c. 700 B.C.).
- He would be without guile. He would do no violence (Isaiah 53:9, c. 700 B.C.).

- He would be rejected by His brethren: "I am become a stranger unto my brethren, and an alien unto my mother's children" (Psalm 69:8, c. 1000 B.C.).
- He would be hated by myriads of people: "They that hate me without a cause are more than the hairs of mine head" (Psalm 69:4, c. 1000 B.C.).
- He would be rejected by the rulers of the Jews: "The stone which the builders rejected has become the chief cornerstone" (Psalm 118:22, c. 1000 B.C), and He is the chief cornerstone of His Church.

POINTS OF IDENTIFICATION

Author Frederich Meldau points out that as few as five simple points of identification can single out any individual from all of the 6 billion other people that live on this planet, and yet with Christ we have 333 points of identification. Think about this: suppose your name is Lester B. Smith, and somewhere in the world an envelope with your name and the address of 4143 Madison Avenue, Chicago, Illinois, U.S.A. is mailed. It does not matter in what country that letter is mailed; it will ultimately come to you because it has the five key points of identification: the country, the state, the city, the street, and your name.

Note that one point alone is not sufficient for identification. A Christian once showed an educated unbeliever one of the 333 Old Testament prophecies concerning Christ. After reading it, the skeptic said that he thought that for purposes of identifying Christ it was very weak and unsatisfactory. The Christian replied, "I agree with you."

"What?" the skeptic exclaimed, "You agree with me?"

"Yes," said the Christian. "I think it is weak and unsatisfactory in the same way that I think a single thread is weak and unsatisfactory to handle any great weight and can be easily snapped. And yet if we take 333 such threads and wind them together, no man, not even the two strongest men we could find, would be able to break the cord produced by the combined threads. So it is with these prophecies. Though any of them may appear to be weak and unsatisfactory in identifying the Messiah, when all of them come together, they present a case which is unbreakable."

Similarly, if I were to take one piece from a box containing a large jigsaw puzzle which, when assembled, featured the face of a famous individual, and I were to say to you, "Oh, I recognize this. It's Abraham Lincoln." You would not be easily convinced. But when all the pieces of the puzzle were in place, the features of our sixteenth President would be clearly delineated and it would be easy for you to recognize him.

Here is my answer to the skeptics who say that one text alone is not enough:

- When you are confronted not with a single obscure text, but by a vast avalanche of texts;
- When you consider that that avalanche is far greater than can be ascribed to chance;
- When you see the specificity of these texts dealing with one single individual—a specificity that startles the mind of even an unbeliever;
- When there is no possibility that these prophecies were written after the events and pawned off as such; (the Old Testament was finished and circulated 400 years before Jesus was born);
- When it is not possible that these predictions could be fulfilled by human cunning because they involve supernatural elements, such as the Virgin Birth and the resurrection from the dead;
- When these prophecies are devoid of that obscurity which so taints the oracles of Delphi or the Sibylline oracle;
- When these prognostications have been written by dozens of different writers with different backgrounds living in different centuries on three different continents

writing in several different languages and they have, nevertheless, woven for us a tapestry which is so intricate and so beautiful as to only have been composed by an artist;

- When they are armed with a power of divine thought, and winged with the most noble of sentiments, electrified by the power of the Holy Spirit;
- When the very person who is so carefully delineated and so minutely detailed in these prophecies steps out of the pages of prophecy and right onto the stage of history...

Then, *you know* that the hand of God has been manifested in your midst and that the finger of God has been writing all of this on the walls of time.

FULFILLED BY JESUS

What do these prophecies absolutely prove beyond any doubt? They prove that Jesus of Nazareth *only* is the person that fulfills all 456 details of the Old Testament prophecies about the coming Messiah. They prove:

- That He is, indeed, the very Christ, the divine Son of God.
- They prove, furthermore, that the Bible, then, is a divine revelation written by the very hand of God.
- And finally, they prove that there is a God who has done all of this, a God who knows the future.

All three of these things are inescapably proven by the prophecies of Christ in the Old Testament. No other religion offers anything vaguely resembling this. We are confronted with such evidence that nothing but the stubborn unbelief of the human heart would cause a person to reject it.

CHANCE OF BEING FULFILLED

What are the chances of one person fulfilling all these prophecies? (Keep in mind we have only read a portion of them.) The late

Peter Stoner, Professor Emeritus of Science at Westmont College, said that this will give you an idea of the chances of one man fulfilling just 48 of the few hundred prophecies concerning the Messiah: If you were to take just one inch of one line of electrons (an electron is the smallest thing we know about—that little thing that goes around the nucleus of an atom) and place them right next to each other, how long would it take for you to count that one inch of electrons? The answer: 19 million years. That is how small they are; we happen to have more of those than anything else in the entire universe.

Imagine that the entire world was packed full of nothing but electrons. Then, let's make this ball larger so it goes out a billion, trillion times farther, until finally we have a ball that is 76 trillion miles in diameter—a solid ball of electrons. That is much larger than the whole solar system. Let's imagine that there were a billion such balls. Now suppose you take a blind friend in a space ship and let him fly around as long as he wants. Finally, he decides to scoop up some electrons. He picks out one, and the one he picks out is the one you somehow marked from the beginning.

If he can find the one you marked, by chance, in a billion balls of electrons bigger than the solar system, then those 48 prophecies could have also happened by chance. These odds are staggering. There is *no way* they were fulfilled by chance. There is *no way* they were written after the event.

Consider these insights from author James C. Hefley:

> A college class in the Pasadena (California) City College applied the laws of probability to the fulfillment of eight Old Testament prophecies concerning the coming of Christ. They concluded:
>
> "(1) birth in Bethlehem (Micah 5:2) one chance in 280,000; (2) a forerunner or messenger would announce His coming (Malachi 3:1) one chance in 1,000; (3) the Messiah would make a triumphant

entry into Jerusalem upon a colt (Zechariah 9:9) one chance in 10,000; (4) He would be betrayed by a friend and suffer wounds (Zechariah 13:6) one chance in 1,000; (5) the betrayer would receive 30 pieces of silver (Zechariah 11:12) one chance in 10,000; (6) the silver would be thrown to a potter (Zechariah 11:13) one chance in 100,000; (7) the Savior, though innocent, would be oppressed and afflicted; He would make no defense (Isaiah 53:7) one chance in 10,000; and (8) He would die by crucifixion (Psalm 22:16) one chance in 10,000."

Based on these estimates, the class figured that the chance of all eight of these prophecies being fulfilled by one person would be the equivalent of 280,000 x 1,000 x 10,000 x 1,000 x 10,000 x 100,000 x 10,000 x 10,000.[9]

In short, the odds are so great that it would be essentially impossible for Jesus *not* to be the Messiah.

INSIGHTS FROM A FORMER ATHEIST

Lee Strobel, a former skeptic, says, of the prophecies Christ fulfilled, that the Old Testament gives us a thumbprint: "It says that when you find the person that fits this thumbprint, that's the Messiah. That's the Son of God, and throughout history, only Jesus Christ has had that thumbprint."[10] Strobel—who earned a law degree at Yale—was an award-winning legal affairs journalist for the *Chicago Tribune* when he was confronted with the claims of Christ. He decided to apply all of his journalistic skills to Christianity, so he could show how historically incorrect it was. But the skeptic became a believer when he studied the facts, as has happened many times throughout history.

If you are a skeptic, I challenge you to study the historical facts about Jesus Christ—His death, His resurrection, and the prophecies written hundreds of years before He came that show with pinpoint accuracy that Christianity is true.

As Lee Strobel studied the prophecies that Jesus fulfilled, he found that they were not easily dismissed. He writes, "The more I studied them, the more difficulty I had in trying to explain them away."[11] As he looked at the odds of any one person fulfilling these prophecies, he was stunned at the scientific evidence that Jesus was the Messiah. Strobel was also shocked by the work of mathematician Peter Stoner,[12] who proved that the chance of any one person fulfilling even eight of these Old Testament prophecies was one in 10^{17} —that is 10 with seventeen zeroes after it. Strobel then began to grapple with the implications of those formidable odds:

> To try to comprehend that enormous number, I did some calculations. I imagined the entire world being covered with white tile that was one-and-a-half inches square—every bit of dry land on the planet—with the bottom of just one tile painted red.
>
> Then I pictured a person being allowed to wander for a lifetime around all seven continents. He would be permitted to bend down only one time and pick up a single piece of tile. What are the odds it would be the one tile whose reverse side was painted red? The odds would be the same as just eight of the Old Testament prophecies coming true in any one person throughout history.[13]

If that did not boggle Strobel's mind enough, Stoner demonstrated that the chances of any one person fulfilling 48 prophecies were one in 10^{157}.[14] Strobel realized the incredible implications of that as well. It would be like finding "a single predetermined atom among all the atoms in a trillion trillion trillion trillion billion universes the size of our universe."[15] Lee Strobel finally did the intellectually honest thing—he recognized Jesus as the Messiah. He has now written such classics as *The Case for Christ* and *The Case for Faith*.

CONCLUSION

This is just the tip of the iceberg of the amazing prophecies that Jesus fulfilled in His first coming. We close this chapter with this remarkable observation of Canon Dyson Hague:

> Who could draw a picture of a man not yet born? Surely God, and God alone. Nobody knew over 500 years ago that Shakespeare was going to be born; or over 250 years ago that Napoleon was to be born. Yet here in the Bible we have the most striking and unmistakable likeness of a Man portrayed, not by one, but by twenty or twenty-five artists, none of whom had ever seen the Man they were painting.[16]

CHAPTER 4

The Skeptics and the Prophecies

෨෮෨

They have Moses and the prophets; let them hear them.
Luke 16:29

Skeptics, of course, do not accept the idea that Jesus fulfilled Messianic prophecies of the Old Testament. For example, Dr. Amy-Jill Levine trains future ministers at Vanderbilt Divinity School. She is Jewish and does not believe that Jesus is the Christ. Here is what she told our television audience in our ground-breaking program, *Who Is This Jesus*:

> Because I'm Jewish I'm often asked, "How come you don't believe in Jesus? He fulfilled all those Messianic prophecies you have back in the Old Testament?" There's actually no Messianic checklist. It's not as if somebody went through and said, you know, born in Bethlehem; mom has to be a virgin; crucified. It's not there.[17]

She also added:

> One might even say, for example, the death of

the Messiah—His torture, His crucifixion—is predicted in the Old Testament. Well, in fact, it's not,
which is why Paul has to walk around explaining,
"Yes, I know, the Cross is a scandal and a folly." People
were not expecting the Messiah to die on a Cross.
We then need to rethink from Christianity's perspective, what then counts as a Messianic prediction.[18]

Why does she not think Jesus fulfills prophecy? In part because
of those predictions He has yet to fulfill:

In my own view, those Messianic prophecies,
which are, to me, essential, are the Messiah is someone who establishes justice throughout the world.
And I look out my window, and I know that hasn't
happened. The Messiah is someone who conquers
death, conquers disease, and I know that hasn't
happened.[19]

Dr. Edwin Yamauchi, a Christian who teaches ancient history at
the University of Miami (Ohio), disagrees:

Not all of the prophecies in the Old Testament
about the Messiah were fulfilled at Jesus' lifetime;
that is, the kingdom of righteousness was not established in Israel, the Jews were not freed from their
Roman oppressors, so forth and so on. Now, the
Christian's answer to that is that those prophecies
will be fulfilled when Christ comes again a second
time in glory."[20]

"THE PASSOVER PLOT"
Dr. Hugh Schonfield was a leading modern skeptic who questioned the notion that Jesus fulfilled Messianic prophecy. In his best-

selling 1965 book, *The Passover Plot*, Schonfield postulates that Jesus, having concluded He was the Messiah, did everything in His life to fulfill prophecies. Of course, it is hard to see how He could have conspired to be born in the tribe of Judah, in the line of David, to a virgin mother, in the town of Bethlehem. But Schonfield dismisses the miraculous out of hand.

Schonfield states:

> For the man who embarked on this formidable and fantastic undertaking, this was no game he was playing. He was in deadly earnest. As he saw it in his own time and setting, with its strange obsessions, tremendous issues depended on the measure of his faithfulness to unalterable divine decrees. He had need of all those qualities of mind and character which had been promised to the Messiah to enable him to succeed.[21]

Schonfield goes on to say that in the last week of Jesus' life, "Jesus had boldly and publicly committed himself in the way he had planned. ... In a masterly way he was bringing it about that the requirements of the Messianic prophecies, as he interpreted them, would be fulfilled."[22]

In the Gospels, Jesus arranged for two of His disciples to go pick up a colt at such and such an address. Schonfield sees this as an example of a secret arrangement Jesus made with just a couple of His followers. He then speculates: Could this not be the same pattern by which Jesus would bring about His death, arrange for His body to be removed to a secret tomb, and be revived with spices and herbs? He argues that maybe Jesus did this with a couple of disciples unbeknownst to other apostles who were not in on the plot: "These stories [like the colt example] show Jesus making secret arrangements in advance with people whom obviously he trusted implicitly, plans which were so vital that he had not disclosed them even to his closest disciples."[23]

So Jesus is not the Master Teacher; He is the master deceiver. For example, Schonfield implies that Jesus worked in tandem with Mary, Martha, and Lazarus to *pretend* to raise Lazarus from the dead. He did this to provoke trouble with the Jews, whose situation in the Roman Empire was precarious.

Furthermore, Jesus conspired with some of His disciples to make it seem like He had really died on the Cross, with plans to revive Him in the tomb and declare Him risen from the dead. Schonfield writes: "Jesus lay in the tomb over the Sabbath. He would not regain consciousness for many hours, and in the meantime the spices and linen bandages provided the best dressing for his injuries."[24] But the Roman soldier who pierced His side ruined the plot by hastening Jesus' death. Schonfield says, "If, as the Fourth Gospel says, his side was pierced by a lance before he was taken from the cross, his chance of recovery was slender."[25]

An interesting irony in Schonfield's book is that he essentially dismisses John's Gospel out of hand as a second century document, which is not true. We know both from Polycarp's testimony and from a small fragment of a copy of John ("the John Rylands Manuscript") that it was written in the first century, as were the other three biblical Gospels. On the one hand, Schonfield dismisses the Gospel of John as untrustworthy; on the other hand, certain incidents in John, e.g, the raising of Lazarus and the lance in Jesus' side, are critical to his thesis.

Schonfield patronizes the early Christians, declaring that most of them were not in on the plot. "There was no deliberate untruth in the witness of the followers of Jesus to his resurrection."[26] Jesus' remains were secretly removed to an unmarked grave. "He had schemed in faith for his physical recovery, and what he expected had been frustrated by circumstances quite beyond his control."[27] Again, the Roman lance foiled the brilliant plot.

So, according to Hugh Schonfield, Jesus was not the prophesied Messiah, but a scheming fraud. What does this say about His character? The Church was founded by the apostles who preached the resurrection. If this skeptical view were right, then at least some of them knew they had stolen the body and planted it in a garden, but they went ahead and proclaimed that He had risen from the dead. This theory not only impugns the character of Jesus and the apostles, it falls way short of explaining historical facts.

Something happened to the disciples that changed them—in a moment—from cowardice to heroic courage. They said the turning point was that they had seen Jesus risen from the dead. To say that they stole Jesus' body and made up the resurrection does not make sense. That view does not reflect the realities of human nature. For example, when two criminals are charged with the same murder, even when they have previously been friends, they will almost invariably accuse the other of pulling the trigger. But the disciples never changed their story one bit, although they had everything to gain and nothing to lose by doing so. The apostles continued throughout all of their lives to proclaim that they had seen Him risen from the dead. Their speaking out led to torture and execution, but not a one ever sought to save his own skin by revealing a "plot."

Dr. Principal Hill wrote *Lectures in Divinity*, which were popular in the nineteenth century and expose the absurdity of these types of theories. Although writing decades before *The Passover Plot*, he raised points that Schonfield's book does not answer:

> You must suppose that twelve men of mean birth, of no education, living in that humble station which placed ambitious views out of their reach and far from their thoughts, without any aid from the state, formed the noblest scheme which ever entered into the mind of man, adopted the most daring means of executing that scheme, conducted it with such address as to conceal the imposture under

the semblance of simplicity and virtue. You must suppose, also, that men guilty of blasphemy and falsehood, united in an attempt the best contrived, and which has in fact proved the most successful for making the world virtuous; that they formed this single enterprise without seeking any advantage to themselves, with an avowed contempt of loss and profit, and with the certain expectation of scorn and persecution; that although conscious of one another's villainy, none of them ever thought of providing for his own security by disclosing the fraud, but that amidst sufferings the most grievous to flesh and blood they persevered in their conspiracy to cheat the world into piety, honesty and benevolence. Truly, they who can swallow such suppositions have no title to object to miracles.[28]

Skeptics like Schonfield have the benefit of looking back on history and seeing the significance of the Christian movement. But the apostles had no such luxury. They were simply witnesses of what they had seen and heard. Skeptics may dismiss the prophecies Jesus fulfilled by assuming—before they look at the facts—that the miraculous is not possible. But even some of the specific things Jesus fulfilled point to circumstances beyond His control.

RESPONDING TO THE SKEPTICS

Dr. Sam Lamerson of Knox Theological Seminary says this about the skeptical scholar who rejects the prophecies because he assumes that the miraculous (in this case, predictive prophecy) does not happen.

[The skeptical scholar] is saying, for instance, that if Matthew talks about Jesus being born in Bethlehem as a prophecy, that Matthew backed into that. He found out that Jesus was born in Bethlehem, he searched through the Old Testament, found a place where it said that the Messiah would be born in Bethlehem and so he backed into it. And therefore, it's not reliable. It becomes, it seems to me, statistically, virtually impossible that the Gospel writers could have backed into all of these prophecies.[29]

Dr. Lamerson further rebuts this liberal argument, citing an example written a millennium before Christ:

In Psalm 22, we have a very clear description of the crucifixion. And virtually all scholars, probably over 99 percent of New Testament scholars will agree that Jesus was crucified. And so then we ask ourselves, "How is it that this Psalm 22, which clearly describes the crucifixion and was seen by many, many Jews as a Messianic Psalm, happens to fit the fact that Jesus, Himself, was crucified?" And we say, "Well, it fits that because that's part of God's redemptive history."[30]

How does Dr. Lamerson understand the skeptics' claims about Jesus and prophecy? He gives an example surrounding Jesus' birth:

In Micah 5:2, we have a description of the Messiah coming from Bethlehem. Matthew quotes that and says, "Jesus was born in Bethlehem." What a John Dominic Crossan and a Robert Funk* would

---

* These two men (one alive, one dead) are very skeptical New Testament scholars. They were the co-founders of the Jesus Seminar, which sat in judgment on the words of Jesus, concluding that He only supposedly said for sure 18 percent of what is attributed to Him in the Gospels.

say is that Jesus really was not born in Bethlehem and that Matthew just made that up. Essentially, they are saying that it is absolutely impossible for any prophecy at all to ever take place. They are saying that as a result of their presupposition, and they are saying, "I'm from the twenty-first century; you have to trust me. You can't trust Matthew who was there and who actually spoke to Jesus. He does not know. I do know."[31]

Dr. Paul Maier is a professor of ancient history at Western Michigan University. He notes:

Jesus fulfilled a whole [series] of Messianic prophecies, as you well know, beginning with little Bethlehem, as the prophet Micah had foretold that it would be in Bethlehem where He shall be born who shall lead His people Israel, and so on. There are numerous others. "Out of Egypt have I called my Son," from the flight to Egypt. Up in Galilee, that He would be preaching liberation to those who were in duress of various kinds. That was Jesus' first commentary when He stood up in the synagogue at Nazareth, you recall. "He shall be called a Nazarene." The details in regard to His passion, death, and resurrection were, of course, all over the Old Testament. In the prophet Isaiah, chapter 53 we have almost a running commentary on what happened on Good Friday to Jesus. A remarkable, remarkable prediction. And so it goes. … I think it would be mathematically impossible for anyone else ever to fulfill all these parameters of prophecy in the Old Testament any better than Jesus did.[32]

"MY PEOPLE, THE JEWS"

Dr. Paul Feinberg, a Jewish believer in Jesus, teaches theology students at Trinity Evangelical Divinity School:

> I have a special love for Jesus because He is the fulfillment of the prophecies to my people, the Jews. And He is a Jew in the most magnificent sense as we see Him on the pages of scripture. As Paul says in the 9th Chapter of Romans, His human ancestry is traced to the people of Israel.[33]

Furthermore, Dr. Lamerson points out:

> Jesus was, indeed, unique in the sense that He fulfilled the prophecies that the Old Testament had set out for Him. The problem, of course, is that in the first century there were lots of "Messiahs." It wasn't just Jesus; there were lots of different kinds of Messianic expectations. And Jesus, in the New Testament, in the Gospels, in Matthew, Mark, and Luke, they say, "This is how we know that Jesus is the Messiah [because He fulfilled Old Testament prophecies]." When you see Paul arguing in the marketplace, he says, "This is how we know Jesus is the Messiah." And he uses Old Testament or Hebrew Bible evidence to say that the Messiah was predicted; these predictions have come true. Jesus, therefore, really is the Messiah, not these other false pretenders.[34]

One of the speculations of some liberal scholars regarding Jesus fulfilling prophecy is the idea that the New Testament writers essentially made things up about Jesus in order to argue that He fulfilled these prophecies. Dr. Yamauchi explains the argument:

Scholars who are skeptical look at the quotation of Old Testament Scriptures, not as confirmation, as Christians do, but rather, as the basis of fabrication. And that of course, takes a very skeptical jaundiced view, which requires a highly inventive imagination on the part of the Gospel writers.[35]

FALSE EXPECTATIONS

Part of what we need to understand about Jesus and prophecies is that the Jewish leaders had built up false expectations as to who the Messiah was going to be and what He was going to do. Dr. N. T. Wright is the Bishop of Durham in England:

We can see this slippage between Jesus' own agenda, why He was going to Jerusalem, and what they thought. … They had very specific ideas about what a prophetical Messianic movement ought to look like and be doing, and though Jesus was doing quite a lot of that stuff, and the healing and the feasting and the celebrating, this is all about the kingdom of God, and the Messianic banquet, and "Yes, great, let's do it." But then, Jesus goes in a different track from where they are expecting Him to go. And that's why they then appear so muddled. And it points up the loneliness of Jesus as He goes to the Cross.[36]

Dr. Wright points out that some of the hypercritics (my term) viewed Jesus as failing in His mission. This wrong view is based on a faulty understanding of His mission:

Scholars, for over 200 years, have been trying to make out in one way or another that Jesus failed, usually because they thought … that Jesus was expecting either a great military victory, or a great divine intervention, or something like that. That is to misunderstand something which is very central to Jesus. … Jesus had plugged into the whole Jewish tradition about martyrdom, about suffering, about going the dark route to the kingdom, rather than the military, glorious [way].[37]

Dr. Wright points out: "A crucified Messiah was a failed Messiah." But because of Jesus' resurrection from the dead, He did not fail. Of course, liberal scholars who deny the atonement of Christ usually reject the resurrection, as they also reject any miracle. If Jesus had not risen from the dead, then He would, indeed, have failed in His mission. Dr. Wright continues:

[W]hen Paul is writing to the Corinthians, which must be dated somewhere between 53 and 56, somewhere in that frame, he says, "Let me remind you what I said right from the beginning, which is the same as what everybody else says. And this is it, that Christ died for our sins, according to the Scriptures, that He was buried, that He was raised on the third day, according to the Scriptures." And he says, "Look, whether it was me telling you this or the other people who you've heard preach, this is the message we all give." Now, that cannot have been dreamt up in the 50s or even in the 40s. That must go back, because that's the whole point of what Paul is saying, to the very, very early days. And already we know from that, because the word "Christ" is a title, not a proper name, we know that this means that from the very beginning, they regarded Jesus as the Messiah. They were interpreting His death in terms of biblical prophecy. ... He'd had a Messianic career, if you like, which had ended in a Scripturally prophesied death and a Scripturally prophesied resurrection. And all of that we got from that one little bit in Paul.[38]

The core message of the Christian faith, that Jesus died for our sins and that He rose from the dead in fulfillment of the Scriptures, has not changed from the very beginning of the Christian Church. Dr. Wright points out that Jesus saw Himself as the fulfillment of the suffering servant strand of Old Testament prophecies:

It seems to me, what's going on with Jesus, is that He soaks himself in the Jewish scriptures and came up with quite a fresh understanding of what the Lord's anointed might actually be supposed to be doing because He made central for His agenda Isaiah 53 and Daniel 7 and several of the Psalms which were not just about the authority that the Messiah would have, though it was that as well, but about the suffering by which He would attain His kingdom.[39]

Dr. Wright sums it all up this way: "Jesus fulfilled a very great deal of Messianic prophecy, yes. But quite a lot of it was fulfilled in ways that people of the time weren't expecting. This is the critical thing."[40]

CONCLUSION

Father Francis Martin teaches at the John Paul II Cultural Institute in Washington, D.C. He observes:

Suppose you were to find a music manuscript, and it contained harmonies to something. And they were brilliant and beautiful passages in there but the whole thing did not make sense. And then came the melodic line and now the whole thing made sense. Jesus is the melodic line to the whole of the Old Testament.[41]

PART TWO

Prophecy/Fulfillment

INTRODUCTION

The purpose of this section is to look at the fulfillment of many specific Old Testament prophecies (not including the book of Isaiah). The reality of these prophecies and fulfillments are like seeing the fingerprints of God.

Some of these chapters are long. Most of them are short.

The format of the following chapters, for the rest of the book, is simple. We begin each chapter with at least two Scripture verses. The first is from the Old Testament (PROPHECY). Then the New Testament (FULFILLMENT) is quoted.

These prophecies begin in Genesis and end in Malachi. From the beginning through the end of the Hebrew Bible, Jesus is seen over and over. A true outline of His life could be based solely on the various facts in the next several chapters—without ever touching the New Testament.

His humanity is foretold—He who is the "seed of a woman." But so also is His divinity foretold. He is both the Son of God and the Son of Man. To Him has been given a kingdom so that people from all tribes and cultures and tongues shall worship Him.

CHAPTER 5

The First Gospel

❦

PROPHECY:
*And I will put enmity between you and the woman, and between
your seed and her Seed; He shall bruise your head,
and you shall bruise His heel.*
Genesis 3:15

FULFILLMENT:
*He who sins is of the devil, for the devil has sinned from the
beginning. For this purpose the Son of God was manifested,
that He might destroy the works of the devil.*
1 John 3:8

In Genesis 3:15, Jesus is first mentioned, as the seed of the
woman. His heel will be bruised by Satan, but He will crush the
devil's head.

Genesis 3:15 is the *protevangelium*. That is, it is the first Gospel.
This is the first time we get a glimpse of the Gospel. The seed of the
woman, while getting injured Himself, will destroy the head of the
serpent. As mentioned earlier, here is the only person in the Bible
who is called the seed of a woman. Other references are always to

Adam and Eve Driven Out of Eden

the seed of a man; it is a man that has produced the child. Jesus was not begotten by any man; He was born of the Virgin Mary.

After they had sinned, Adam and Eve clothed themselves in fig leaf aprons of their own making. People have been doing this ever since because one of the results of the fall was, first of all, shame at their nakedness. Man retains the element of shame because of his sin, and he tries to cover himself up. In this case, the fig leaves of his own self-righteousness, his own piety, morality, churchgoing, commandment keeping, benevolence, or whatever it is; they are all fig leaves, and they will not cover his shame and nakedness.

We then read that God made a coat of skins and covered man with them—an adumbration of the great covering that God would provide in His own Son, the Lamb of God, who would be slain and rise again to clothe us with the white robes of His own perfect righteousness.

Through Christ, we can be given a new nature—a nature that does, indeed, love God and love our neighbor, a nature that desires to do good unto mankind. It is through the power of the Gospel and the regenerating power of the Holy Spirit that there is any hope for any of us, for this nation, and for this world. It is a glorious hope, and it is a hope that is promised and foreshadowed for us right here in the third chapter of Genesis.

CONCLUSION

The whole Bible can be described in just three words: *generation, degeneration, regeneration. Generation* in chapters one and two of Genesis, *degeneration* in chapter three, and *regeneration*—the story of all of the rest of the Bible. If we don't understand the fall of man, we will never understand redemption.

CHAPTER 6

The One Who Blesses the Whole World

❧

PROPHECY
I will bless those who bless you [Abraham], and I will curse him who curses you; and in you all the families of the earth shall be blessed.
Genesis 12:3

FULFILLMENT
... Jesus Christ, the Son of David, the Son of Abraham.
Matthew 1:1

And the Scripture, foreseeing that God would justify the Gentiles by faith, preached the gospel to Abraham beforehand, saying, "In you all the nations shall be blessed".... Now to Abraham and his Seed were the promises made. He does not say, "And to seeds," as of many, but as of one, "And to your Seed," who is Christ.
Galatians 3:8, 16

We are told in Genesis 12 that through Abraham the entire world would be blessed. Jesus fulfilled this. The whole world has been blessed not only by His coming, but also by His followers, who have done so much to change the world for good.

THE ABRAHAMIC COVENANT

In all of recorded history, over thirty men have claimed to be the Jewish Messiah. Yet only Jesus and His teachings have clearly blessed all the nations of the world. He alone, of the over thirty claimants to the Abrahamic throne, fulfills the covenant of blessing that God decreed to Abraham.

Jesus was the fulfillment of the promised seed through which not only Israel, but also all nations, would receive the blessings of God. In Him, the penalty for sin was canceled, and through His resurrection, the powers of this world defeated. His disciples were instructed to take this message of redemption and victory to all the world, that men might believe and be saved (Matthew 28:19–20).

Beginning as only a small band of 120 devoted followers in Jerusalem, these disciples spread the message of Christ that has transformed the world. By the power of His descended Spirit, millions upon millions from every nation and tribe have experienced the new birth.

Through the power of Christ's love, the forces of ungodly civilization—infanticide, abortion, illiteracy, prejudice, treachery, idolatry, polygamy, promiscuity, homosexuality, and tyranny—can be routed. Wherever the Gospel message has been taught and believed, a new dawning of love, humanity, freedom, justice, and peace has appeared. Cannibalism has ceased because of Christianity. No other movement in all history has brought about more substantial gains for mankind—intellectually, morally, and politically—than the advancement and maturation of the Christian faith.[42]

CONCLUSION

Each of us must stand in awe of this great fulfillment of God's promised conquest. Through Christ and His love, God has truly blessed the nations. Indeed, each day and each hour, the Kingdom of God and of Christ continues to grow in strength and power. At times the forces of unbelief and sin raise their monstrous heads, but they cannot stop the inevitable advance of Christ and the impact of His life and resurrection. So, let us pray that God will open wide the door to evangelism around the world—that all men, all cultures, all nations, all peoples might be blessed by the great and merciful Messiah, Jesus.

CHAPTER 7

Isaac: A Reflection of the Coming Christ

∞

PROPHECY

Then God said: "No, Sarah your wife shall bear you a son, and you shall call his name Isaac; I will establish My covenant with him for an everlasting covenant, and with his descendants after him."
Genesis 17:19

For Sarah conceived and bore Abraham a son in his old age, at the set time of which God had spoken to him.
Genesis 21:2

FULFILLMENT

... Jesus ... the son of Jacob, the son of Isaac, the son of Abraham....
Luke 3:23–34

[Abraham] who, contrary to hope, in hope believed, so that he became the father of many nations, according to what was spoken, "So shall your descendants be." And not being weak in faith, he did not consider his own body, already dead (since he was about a hundred years old), and the deadness of Sarah's womb. He did not waver at the promise of God through unbelief, but was strengthened in faith, giving glory to God....
Romans 4:18–20

"Impossible. Absolutely impossible." This feeling must have overwhelmed Abraham when God revealed to him that Sarah would bear a son. So astonishing did this revelation sound that Abraham "fell on his face and laughed, and said in his heart, 'Shall a child be born to a man that is one hundred years old? And shall Sarah, who is ninety years old, bear a child?'" (Genesis 17:17).

So it seemed by human reasoning. Who would believe that a child could be born to a couple so long past childbearing years?

Twice Abraham devised "natural" means to accomplish God's purpose. First, he felt that God's promise could be accomplished through the adoption of Eliezer, his steward. Scripture indicates that Abraham believed that this man, as his adopted son, could fulfill God's promise and bring forth a nation. However, God made it clear this was not His intention—that there would be a child by natural descent from Abraham through which the promises of God would be fulfilled (Genesis 15:1–6).

The second strategy that Abraham and Sarah implemented to accomplish God's promise was much more desperate. Sarah gave Hagar, her handmaiden, to Abraham in accordance with the customs of that time. Through this union, Hagar gave birth to a boy named Ishmael. Abraham hoped that this child would be acceptable to God as the heir of His promises.

However, God again rejected this "human solution" (Genesis 17). Although God blessed Ishmael, He did not allow him to become the heir to the covenant promises.

This privilege was reserved for Isaac, born of Sarah according to the Word of God. When God awakened Sarah's womb and brought about the miracle of Isaac, He demonstrated that He did not need the help of man to accomplish His plan of redemption. He alone would bring salvation, according to His perfect plan and purpose.

With the birth of Isaac, God's plan must have seemed complete. However, God spoke to Abraham, not with subjective inward promptings, but with an audible and real voice, commanding him to sacrifice his son, the son of promise.

The Trial of Abraham's Faith

Abraham's response seems startling. Without protest, he led his son to the mountain of sacrifice. How could this father, who loved his son, willingly take his life? How could God, who is holy, demand this of Abraham?

This entire drama must be placed within the context of the entire biblical revelation. Abraham was no ordinary father; he was a chosen and unique prophet of God who engaged in verbal and objective conversations with the Almighty. Prior to the close of the New Testament canon, God chose special people, like Abraham, to communicate His message.

God had revealed to Abraham that through Isaac, and Isaac only, would the fulfillment of His promises come. Therefore, as Abraham journeyed with Isaac to the mountain ranges of Moriah, he was confident that his boy would not die before God had provided him with descendants who would form a great nation. Abraham believed so strongly in God's promise that he knew, if necessary, God would raise Isaac physically from the dead in order to fulfill His Word (Hebrews 11:17–19). Thus was Abraham's faith. Of course, God stopped the sacrifice of Isaac. He did not have Abraham go through with it, nor had He intended it; it was a test of Abraham's faith all along.

Yet the story is not only about the faith of Abraham; it is also a preview of a future sacrifice—of the promised descendant of Isaac. Abraham even spoke prophetically, declaring that God Himself would provide a lamb. Jesus was that Lamb.

CONCLUSION

Even as Abraham was willing to sacrifice his son, so God, the Father, sacrificed His only begotten Son to redeem man (John 3:16). God provided salvation at incalculable cost to Himself. The "greater Isaac" came as promised and offered His life on a mountain outside of Jerusalem. That mountain became the place of sacrifice for the Lamb that God Himself provided.

CHAPTER 8

Curse Turned to Blessing

❦

PROPHECY
*"I see Him, but not now; I behold Him, but not near; a Star shall
come out of Jacob; a Scepter shall rise out of Israel, and batter the
brow of Moab, and destroy all the sons of tumult. ... Out of Jacob One
shall have dominion, and destroy the remains of the city."*
Numbers 24:17, 19

FULFILLMENT
*The book of the genealogy of Jesus Christ, the Son of David, the Son of
Abraham: Abraham begot Isaac, Isaac begot Jacob, and Jacob begot
Judas and his brothers.*
Matthew 1:1–2

*"I, Jesus, have sent My angel to testify to you these things in the
churches. I am the Root and the Offspring of David, the Bright and
Morning Star."*
Revelation 22:16

*We also have the prophetic word confirmed, which you do well to heed
as a light that shines in a dark place, until the day dawns and the
morning star rises in your hearts....*
2 Peter 1:19

This Old Testament prophecy (cited in the prologue, "Star of Wonder") concerning the Christ is found in one of the most unique chapters in the Bible. Balaam, a pagan prophet renowned for proclaiming God's blessing and curse, had been promised great reward by Balak, King of the Moabites, if he would curse Israel, an enemy Balak feared and hated.

In Numbers 24, Balaam's final attempt to curse Israel is recorded. Twice before, his efforts to curse Israel had failed. Instead, God had caused him to proclaim a blessing. In this last prophecy of Balaam, he not only blessed Israel, but spoke of what would happen in the "latter days."

God revealed through Balaam that from Jacob's descendants and from the nation of Israel would come a great individual who would defeat and destroy all the enemies of God's people. This "Star out of Jacob" would deliver Israel and provide her with perfect security.

The Qumran sect, a devoted group of Jews who lived in a desert community during the time of Christ and devoted themselves to the study and preservation of the Scriptures, recognized in this passage a reference to the Messiah. However, because He did not physically destroy the Roman Empire, they failed to understand that Jesus was the fulfillment of this prophecy for God's people.

The problem for the Qumran sect—and for all Judaism—is that they do not comprehend that in rising from the dead, Christ Jesus has defeated Satan, the ultimate enemy of God's people. He has vanquished the power of sin and death. In 1 Corinthians 15, Paul speaks of over 500 people who personally saw Jesus Christ after His crucifixion. He instructed them concerning the true nature of God's Kingdom and provided infallible proofs that He had been physically resurrected. Jesus Christ's resurrection from the dead demonstrates that all authority has now been given to Him by God the Father, in fulfillment of the Messianic promise.

Jesus is God's great "Rising Star," raised from the dead to be the anointed prophet, priest, and king of God. Revelation 22:16 clearly

The Angel Appearing to Balaam

identifies Jesus as the "Bright Morning Star." Here, the figure of the star is used metaphorically to speak of a divine ruler who would govern the earth in peace. In the ancient world, a star was often used as a representation of deity and angelic powers and, therefore, is a fitting symbol of the divine Messiah (Acts 7:43; Matthew 2:2–10; Revelation 6:13).

Clearly, we must look to Christ as our guiding star, just as the wise men were led to Bethlehem by the miraculous light that appeared in the night sky.

CONCLUSION

In His earthly ministry, His first coming, Jesus fulfilled His role as prophet and priest. In His second coming, He will be seen by the whole world as the rightful King and divine ruler.

CHAPTER 9

The Lion of Judah

❧

PROPHECY
*"The scepter shall not depart from Judah, nor a lawgiver from
between his feet, until Shiloh comes; and to Him shall be the obedience
of the people."*
Genesis 49:10

FULFILLMENT
*[Jesus being] the son of Amminadab, the son of Ram, the son of
Hezron, the son of Perez, the son of Judah,....*
Luke 3:33

*"When the Son of Man comes in His glory, and all the holy angels
with Him, then He will sit on the throne of His glory. All the nations
will be gathered before Him, and He will separate them one from another, as a shepherd divides his sheep from the goats."*
Matthew 25:31

In Genesis 49, we are told that Jesus will come from Judah's line. He will be likened to a lion. To paraphrase C. S. Lewis, like a lion, He may be not be "safe" or "tame," but He is good. The genealogy of Jesus is important, as is the fact that all the genealogical records in Jerusalem were destroyed in A.D. 70 by the Romans. Therefore, there could be *no* Messiah (a man who would be definitely Jewish, of David's lineage, etc.), after A.D. 70.

JACOB'S PREDICTION

Before Jacob died, he blessed his children. When he came to Judah, he made the incredible promise regarding the lion of Judah. God's promise to the house of Judah, of royal power and civil rule, was initially attained in the Davidic kingship and the Davidic covenant (2 Samuel 7:16). However, the climax of this prophecy was scheduled for fulfillment when "Shiloh"—God's "establisher of peace"—would appear (Genesis 49:10).

It is amazing to see the intricate nature of God's plan for world peace unfold in the prophecies of the Old Testament. Most Christians, when reading the Bible, skip over the long lists of genealogies without giving them any thought. I know this because that is what I did as a young Christian. Yet consider for a moment God's intention in providing this historical data. In essence, He provided us with a detailed flowchart of the Messianic promise as it coursed through history—and a clear proof of His power and sovereignty.

To recap a few key prophecies: God first shared His promise of a Messiah in Genesis, when He revealed that the seed of a woman would crush the head of the "serpent." Later, God further defined this prophecy, limiting it to a descendant of Abraham. Of Abraham's sons, God chose Isaac to be the bearer of the Messianic promise and expanded the revelation concerning the mission and task of the Divine Redeemer. In turn, Jacob was selected from Isaac's offspring as the inheritor of God's promise. Now, in this passage, God set apart Judah from his eleven brothers as the only God-ordained line of rulers, until the "establisher of peace" would come.

Jacob Wrestling with the Angel

Through all of this, it is clear that God is directing the course of history toward the eventual appearance of His chosen deliverer. His definite and specific prophecies eliminate all would-be impostors to the Messianic throne. Only Jesus of Nazareth fulfills every detail foretold by the prophets of God. He is God's "Shiloh," the establisher of peace.

At His birth, the angels proclaimed peace to all men who have been favored by God (Luke 2:14). Through His death on the Cross, Jesus came and established peace between God and man (Romans 5:1–5). He also bequeathed to His followers an inner peace of the spirit and a loving peace among the community of faith (Philippians 2:1–4; 4:8–9). Though this peace often would be disturbed by those who rejected Him, nevertheless He would continue to grant His Church internal strength and calm in the midst of persecution and tribulation (Matthew 10:34). Ultimately, through the preaching of the Gospel, the ministry of the Spirit, and His triumphal return in power, universal peace will be established (Isaiah 2:1–6).

CONCLUSION

The genealogy of Jesus shows that Jesus was the descendent of Abraham. In fact, it begins with the statement "Abraham begot Isaac" (Matthew 1:2). Second, it shows that He was also of the tribe of Judah. This was very important, because in Genesis 49 the prophecy was made that, "The scepter shall not depart from Judah, nor a lawgiver from between his feet, until Shiloh comes." (Shiloh is a name for the Messiah.) Not only must Shiloh come through the tribe of Judah, but He must come before the scepter departs from Judah, before their legal authority as a tribe is removed. (Part III of this book will address the genealogies of Jesus in more detail.)

Thus, Jesus is of the seed of Abraham. He is of the tribe of Judah, He is David's greater Son, and this was foretold hundreds of years before it came to pass.

CHAPTER 10

The Prophet

❦

PROPHECY:

"The Lord your God will raise up for you a Prophet like me from your midst, from your brethren. Him you shall hear…"
Deuteronomy 18:15

FULFILLMENT:

"[A]nd that He may send Jesus Christ, who was preached to you before, whom heaven must receive until the times of restoration of all things, which God has spoken by the mouth of all His holy prophets since the world began. For Moses truly said to the fathers, 'The Lord your God will raise up for you a Prophet like me from your brethren. Him you shall hear in all things, whatever He says to you.'"
Acts 3:20–22

Moses was the greatest leader of the Old Testament era. All prophets looked to him as the great revealer of God's will and Word. Yet Moses gave Israel hope that another great prophet would arise. The prophet would bring God's final revelation to man (Hebrews 1:1–3).

Moses Coming Down From Mount Sinai

The Jews, during the time of Christ, were waiting for the appearance of this prophet. They even asked John the Baptist if he was "the second Moses," to which he answered no. Still, this demonstrates that the Jews understood this passage to be prophetic in nature. Stephen later informs us that Jesus of Nazareth was, in fact, the long-awaited Prophet of God. (Acts 7:37)

Moses said that this great Prophet would be like him in many ways. Yet, how was Jesus like Moses? Because Moses was a type of Christ, there are many parallels between him and Jesus Christ. I have summarized these in the following chart.

MOSES	JESUS
1. Life spared in infancy (Exodus 2:1–10).	1. Life spared in infancy (Matthew 2:13–15).
2. Left the royal court to serve his people (Hebrews 11:24–26).	2. Left the royal courts of Heaven to serve His people (John 3:13).
3. He was faithful as a servant (Hebrews 3:2).	3. He was faithful as a servant (Hebrews 3:2).
4. He was full of compassion and love (Numbers 27:17).	4. He was full of compassion and love (Matthew 9:36).
5. An intercessor for his people (Deuteronomy 9:18).	5. An intercessor for God's people (Hebrews 7:25).
6. Revealed the glory of God (2 Corinthians 3:7).	6. Revealed the glory of the only begotten of the Father (John 1:14).
7. A revealer of God's will (Deuteronomy 6:1).	7. A final revealer of God's will (Revelation 1:1).
8. A mediator of the covenant (Deuteronomy 29:1).	8. A mediator of the new covenant (Hebrews 8:6–7).
9. The mediator of the law (Exodus 20).	9. The lawgiver (Matthew 5–7).
10. Led God's people to deliverance (Exodus 14-15).	10. Brought deliverance and salvation from sin (Hebrews 12:1–4).

From this comparison, we can see how Christ fulfilled Moses' prophecy. The law was given through Moses; grace and truth came through Jesus Christ (John 1:17). Jesus completed all which Moses spoke of and shed the full light of God's revelation upon the Old Testament. Only in the light of Christ can the prophecies of Moses and the other Old Testament prophets be clearly understood.

CONCLUSION

Jesus was also a prophet in that He predicted the future, e.g., the fall of Jerusalem, which took place in 70 A.D. He predicted the end times and His Second Coming. He predicted Peter's denial and also His own death and resurrection. He was a prophet in word and deed, as well as *the* Prophet.

CHAPTER 11

The Son of God
The Deity of Christ, Part 1

⊗

PROPHECY:
*"I will declare the decree: The Lord has said to Me, 'You are My Son,
today I have begotten You.'"*
Psalm 2:7

FULFILLMENT:
*"God has fulfilled this for us their children, in that He has raised up
Jesus. As it is also written in the second Psalm: 'You are My Son,
today I have begotten You.'"*
Acts 13:33

The Deity of Jesus Christ was foretold in the Old Testament as
well as many other aspects of His life. Because the subject is so
important, we have devoted three chapters to it, beginning with
this one.

THE CORONATION OF CHRIST
At first glance, Psalm 2:7 seems to be referring to Christ's birth.
Yet, when we read Paul's explanation of these verses in the New

Christ in the Synagogue

Testament, he applies them to the resurrection. How can this be? Where did Paul get the idea of a resurrection from a passage that speaks of a Son being "begotten?"

The key to understanding Paul's interpretation of this verse is found when we recognize that it is cradled in a passage which appears to have been used in the coronation ceremonies of the Davidic kings. During these ceremonies, God symbolically called the new king a "Son." The reason he received this title from God was that the king represented God's covenant faithfulness and the Almighty's rule over Israel. In that light, Paul's use of this verse indicates that it was at the resurrection that Jesus was crowned as God's Messianic King. This happened after His ascension, when He came home in triumph and was seated at the right hand of the Father.

Like much of prophetic literature, the second Psalm blends an historical prediction and Messianic promise. This Psalm is based on God's promise to King David that he would have a Son who would be given a great kingdom by God. Historically, this prophecy was first fulfilled in the rule of King Solomon. Yet, the complete realization occurred when Jesus was awarded the Messianic throne.

Here is the second Psalm in its entirety:

> Why do the nations rage
>   and the peoples plot in vain?
> The kings of the earth set themselves,
>   and the rulers take counsel together,
>   against the LORD and against his anointed,
>   saying, "Let us burst their bonds apart
>   and cast away their cords from us."
> He who sits in the heavens laughs;
>   the LORD holds them in derision.
> Then he will speak to them in his wrath,
>   and terrify them in his fury, saying,
>   "As for me, I have set my King
>   on Zion, my holy hill."
> I will tell of the decree:
>   The LORD said to me, "You are my Son;
>   today I have begotten you.
> Ask of me, and I will make the nations your heritage,
>   and the ends of the earth your possession.

You shall break them with a rod of iron
   and dash them in pieces like a potter's vessel."
Now therefore, O kings, be wise;
   be warned, O rulers of the earth.
Serve the LORD with fear,
   and rejoice with trembling.
Kiss the Son,
   lest he be angry, and you perish in the way,
   for his wrath is quickly kindled.
Blessed are all who take refuge in him (ESV).

This is, undoubtedly, one of the clearest Old Testament passages describing the work and ministry of the Messiah. In it, we are fore-warned that the kings of the earth will take counsel together to disrupt the plans of God's "anointed." This prophecy was fulfilled by the actions of Herod, Pontius Pilate, and the Jewish leaders, leading to the crucifixion of Jesus. All nations, both Jewish and Gentile, conspired to put an end to the Messianic claims of Jesus Christ (Acts 4:26).

In another sense, one could argue that this sort of anti-Christian bigotry and persecution goes on in our own day. In our context, we see a war against anything Christian in the public arena; but in some countries, Christians are killed for their faith. Yet all of these anti-Christian rulers are warned to "kiss the Son," i.e., to pay Him homage. None of their attempts to stop the kingdom of Heaven will succeed.

A classic example of this took place about 300 years after Christ. A Roman emperor, Diocletian, was a terrible persecutor of the faith. He was one of the worst of the emperors who tried to stop the Christian movement. He not only had Christian Scriptures gathered up and burned, he had Christians killed because they were Christians. It was as if Diocletian was saying, "You can worship Jesus Christ—over my dead body." After his reign, Constantine became the emperor and declared Christianity legal. Meanwhile, Diocletian's grave became the cornerstone of a church. For centuries now, Christians have worshiped in that building—if you will—over Diocletian's dead body. No human can stop the Kingdom of God.

Psalm 2 also points out God's attitude toward such intrigues. God is pictured as laughing with scorn at these vain attempts to frustrate His eternal and unchangeable plan of redemption. The rulers of the earth desired to be free of God's rule; yet, God in His power and sovereignty used their rebellion to fulfill His purpose of salvation and establish His Kingdom (Acts 4:28).

Though men killed Jesus in an attempt to escape the rule of the Almighty, God raised Him from the dead and set Him upon David's throne as the chosen and eternal Son. Jesus, as the Divine Prince, was inaugurated, crowned, and given the Kingdom by His Father on Ascension Day.

CONCLUSION

Jesus fulfilled Old Testament prophecy by His resurrection and ascension into Heaven. As Christians, we must understand the great significance of this for our spiritual lives. Because of this act of divine power in history, we have been made partakers in His Kingdom (Ephesians 2).

The power of the resurrection is at work in us to transform our character into the image of Christ and cause God to be glorified by our lives (Ephesians 1:19–23). The crucifixion, resurrection, and ascension stand as the bedrock of our Christian faith and as an historical landmark, declaring the victory of Jesus Christ to all mankind (1 Corinthians 15:57).

CHAPTER 12

The Son of Man
The Deity of Christ, Part 2

※

PROPHECY:

"I was watching in the night visions, and behold, One like the Son of Man, coming with the clouds of heaven! He came to the Ancient of Days, and they brought Him near before Him. Then to Him was given dominion and glory and a kingdom, that all peoples, nations, and languages should serve Him. His dominion is an everlasting dominion, which shall not pass away, and His kingdom the one which shall not be destroyed."
Daniel 7:13–14

FULFILLMENT:

Again the high priest asked Him, saying to Him, "Are You the Christ, the Son of the Blessed?" Jesus said, "I am. And you will see the Son of Man sitting at the right hand of the Power, and coming with the clouds of heaven."
Mark 14:61-62

Jesus' favorite title for Himself was the "Son of Man." In Daniel 7, we read the incredible job description of this "Man" with divine origins, the Heaven-sent go-between who is God's emissary on earth.

JESUS' CLAIM TO DEITY

You often hear skeptics say, "Well, after all, Jesus never claimed to be God or claimed to be the Messiah. So why are you making such a fuss about that?" It's very interesting. Stop and think for a moment. Suppose Jesus had begun His ministry on the first day by walking into the temple and saying, "I am the Messiah. I am your God. Fall down and worship Me." What do you think would have happened? We would have had a premature crucifixion, Jesus Christ would have had no ministry, and all of His marvelous teaching would never have been given. It was imperative that Christ conceal, to some degree—until the appropriate time, until His hour had come—His true identity.

You say, "But He did clearly state early on that He was the Messiah." You're right. In John 4:25-26, He is talking to the Samaritan woman at the well and the woman finally is brought to the place of saying, "I know that Messiah is coming" (who is called Christ). "When He comes, He will tell us all things." Jesus said to her, "I who speak to you am He." That is about as clear-cut a statement as you can possibly get. So why did He come out very clearly and say that very early on? Stop and think. Do you think that woman was going to crucify him? Was He in Jerusalem? Were there scribes and Pharisees and priests around? No, He was in Samaria, where neither a scribe nor a Pharisee would place one foot or even a toe. So He did make clear his Messiahship early on there.

But when He was among the Jews, He both concealed and revealed very tantalizingly who He was, and they often said, "If You are the Christ, tell us plainly." Jesus answered them, "I told you, and you do not believe."

"Well, come out and tell us plainly. Are you or are you not the Christ?"

He replied, "I've already told you and you believe Me not." He would never quite say it, but, the clear statement of the fact that He was the Messiah, the Christ, is seen right there from His own lips (John 4:26).

We are looking at the question: Did Jesus claim to be God? Did He claim to be deity, or did He not, as many a skeptic has said? For the reasons just enumerated, Jesus did not simply say "I am God," but He said it in many, many different ways, and we want to look at those. For example, He claimed all of the attributes of deity.

First, God is omnipresent. That is one of the attributes of deity. Jesus claimed omnipresence. We read in Matthew 18:20, "where two or three are gathered together in my name, there am I in the midst of them." Jesus is right here. He is in a secret gathering of Christians in Libya right now. He is in the underground Church in North Korea. He is in Oman. He is in Belarus. He is everywhere two or three are gathered together in millions of places this day and every day. Christ is present everywhere. He did not even say "there I will be" —but "there I am."

Then, in Matthew 28:19-20, He said, "Go therefore and make disciples of all the nations ... and lo, I am with you always, even to the end of the age." So, as Christ, the apostles, and others went out to proclaim the Gospel, thousands of missionaries and millions of Christians have gone to share the Gospel of Christ. They have gone out crossing every ocean, penetrating every jungle, climbing every mountain, crossing every desert, and wherever they have gone Christ has been with them.

David Livingstone plunged into the deepest darkest jungles of Africa, basing his whole soul upon that text: "Lo, I am with you always even unto the end of the world." He said, "It is the word of a gentleman of the strictest order and there's an end to it." But it is even more than that: it is clearly a word of declaration of omnipresence; it is a statement of God. He said to Nicodemus in John 3:13,

"No one has ascended to heaven but He who came down from heaven, that is, the Son of Man who is in heaven." He was talking to Nicodemus in Jerusalem at the time, but while talking to Nicodemus in Jerusalem, He declared that He was in Heaven, so Christ clearly declared that He was omnipresent.

Second, He claimed that His home was Heaven, that He came from Heaven, and that He had been there before the world began. Notice the indications of that claim. He says in John 6:62, "What then if you should see the Son of Man ascend where He was before?" Which one of you readers was in Heaven before? Which of you remembers anything of an existence before you came forth from your mother's womb? Which one of you was here before the world began? Later, in John 16:28 and 17:5, He says, "I came forth from the Father and have come into the world. Again, I leave the world and go to the Father.... And now, O Father, glorify Me with Yourself, with the glory which I had with You before the world was." Here He claims eternality—that He existed and shared glory with the Father before the world began. This is clearly a claim of deity.

Third, He claimed all knowledge. Is God omniscient? So Christ claims the same. He says, "No one knows the Son except the Father. Nor does anyone know the Father except the Son, and the one to whom the Son wills to reveal Him" (Matthew 11:27). In Revelation 2:23, He says, "I am He who searches the minds and hearts." He says, "Heaven and earth will pass away, but My words will by no means pass away" (Matthew 24:35). The Lord knows all things, and He knows the hearts of men. Christ clearly claimed to have all knowledge. Again, one of the attributes of deity.

Fourth, He claimed omnipotence. In John 5:21, He said, "[A]s the Father raises the dead and gives life to them, even so the Son gives life to whom He will." Is that not a claim to omnipotence? Suppose I walk into a cemetery and say that I am going to raise up whomsoever I will—and then I do? This is a claim of omnipotence, and Jesus made that claim. He said "I and My Father are one" in John 10:30, clearly a statement claiming the omnipotence of the Father.

Fifth, He claimed to own and be Lord of the angels. Did you ever think about that? He said in Matthew 13:41, "The Son of Man will send out His angels." Would any one of us dare claim that the angels are our own, and that we send them to do our bidding? Would you make such a claim as that? Of course not. Yet we accept such self-assertions on the part of Christ because they are perfectly natural. He is able to do and is, by His character, all that He says that He can do and is.

Sixth, He claims to be the judge. Is the Father the Judge of all of the earth? So is the Son. We read in Matthew 25:31, 32, 46, these words,

> When the Son of Man comes in His glory, and all the holy angels with Him, then He will sit on the throne of His glory. All the nations will be gathered before Him, and He will separate them one from another, as a shepherd divides his sheep from the goats. … And these will go away into everlasting punishment, but the righteous into eternal life.

"For the Father judges no one, but has committed all judgment to the Son" (John 5:22). So we see that the divine prerogative of judgment which, in the Old Testament, is repeatedly declared about God, has been referred to God the Son as the Judge of all of the earth. All nations will come before Him, and Christ will declare who goes into Heaven and who goes into Hell. That is definitely a claim of deity.

Seventh, we see that He allows Himself to be called Lord and God. In John 20:28 we read, "And Thomas answered and said to Him, 'My Lord and my God!'"

Chances are, you may talk to Jehovah's Witnesses sometime, and they like to try to get rid of John 1:1. They claim that when it says, "and the Word was God," it does not have the definite Greek article before it so, therefore, it should be translated "the Word was *a* God."

That is hogwash, and it is the kind of statement made by people who do not have a clue as to what the Greek language means at all. They do not understand certain verb tenses in the Greek, so they make up stupid things like that to confuse the gullible and uninformed.

One time I spoke with a woman from that group, and we got talking, and lo and behold, we started talking about the deity of Christ. I said that we believe that Jesus was God, and she said, "Well, no, the Bible never teaches that."

And I said, "Well, the Bible says 'In the beginning was the Word, and the Word was with God, and the Word was God.'"

And she said "Oh well, it doesn't say that in the Greek." Now here was a woman that I do not think ever got through high school, and she's telling people what the Greek says. It's their favorite ploy—to deceive people that do not know.

So I replied, "Is that right?"

She said, "Oh yes, it doesn't say that in the Greek."

I said, "I'm amazed." I then told her what the statement is in the Greek.

She said, "What?"

I said "I thought that's what it said in the Greek." I just happened to have my Greek New Testament with me, so I asked her, "Would you show me where it says what you said that it says?"

She took my Greek New Testament, and as God is my witness, she opened it up sideways, started looking at it, and said, "What is this?"

"That's the Greek New Testament. You were going to show me where it says that Jesus isn't God."

She said, "What is this?" I said, "That's the Greek New Testament." She turned it upside down; she tried to read it that way. She said again, "What is this?"

I again said, "That is the Greek New Testament. Now, you were going to show me something in there."

Then she turned it on its side and tried to read it that way, and

Jesus and the Woman at the Well

said, "What *is* this?"

I said, "My dear lady, that is the New Testament in the original Greek language, and you were telling me what it said. I would just like for you to show me that. You've been all around the neighborhood here telling people what the Greek New Testament says. So I just thought that you could show me where it says that."

She had no more knowledge of Greek than a parrot in a cage saying "Polly wants a cracker." She was just parroting things that they had told her and had no idea what they really meant.

All of that to say that in *this* text in John 20:28, where Thomas said "my Lord and my God," the definite Greek article is present. What it says in Greek, then, is "the Lord and the God of me." It could not possibly be clearer than that.

Moving on to point eight: Only God forgives sin. Jesus claims to have the power to forgive sin. In Luke 7:48 He says, "Your sins are forgiven." Then, in Matthew 9:2 we read, "When Jesus saw their faith, He said to the paralytic, 'Son, be of good cheer; your sins are forgiven you.'" Do you remember that the Pharisees that were there murmured among themselves saying, "Who has the power to forgive sins except God only? This man blasphemes."

Matthew continues, "But Jesus, knowing their thoughts, said, 'Why do you think evil in your hearts? For which is easier, to say, 'Your sins are forgiven you,' or to say, 'Arise and walk?' But that you may know that the Son of Man has power on earth to forgive sins'— then He said to the paralytic, 'Arise, take up your bed, and go to your house.'"

And, to the astonishment of all, this paralyzed man stood up, took up his bed, and walked out of the room in the midst of gaping mouths. So Jesus clearly claimed to have the power to forgive sin, but the Jews clearly declared that no one but God has the power to forgive sins. Jesus, therefore, demonstrated that He was God. That is a claim and a demonstration of deity.

Jesus also made many silent claims of deity. Teddy Roosevelt said, "Walk softly and carry a big stick." You do not necessarily have to say how powerful you are. If you walk into a gymnasium where the world champion heavyweight weight lifters are getting ready for the Olympics, there are several things you can do. You can say, "I am stronger than all of these men." People would probably laugh. On the other hand, you can walk up and watch some Bulgarian, who is just trying to lift 650 pounds and is not able to get it up and drops it to the floor with a crash. Then you reach down with one hand and pick it up and put it down again. Do you have to say anything? Do you have to say, "I am stronger than any of the other men in this room?" Of course not.

"Teacher, do You not care that we are perishing?" cried the disciples when Jesus was asleep in the back of the boat and a great storm had suddenly come down upon the Sea of Galilee. Jesus stood up, rebuked the waves and the wind, and suddenly the winds ceased and the waves fell silent at His feet. "And they feared exceedingly, and said to one another, 'Who can this be, that even the wind and the sea obey Him!'" (Mark 4:41). Now that was a non-verbal claim to deity. Often, those can be more powerful than mere verbal statements. So Jesus made the claim to deity not only with His mouth—but with His deeds as well.

Number nine. He claimed to be the Lord of the Sabbath. Now to the Jews, the Sabbath was a very, very important thing. They were Sabbatarians of the strictest kind. I am afraid that we have gone much too far in the opposite direction. Jesus said, "For the Son of Man is Lord even of the Sabbath" (Matthew 12:8). To be "the Lord of the Sabbath" is an incredible claim. "I am the Lord of Tuesday." What a claim for anyone to declare that He is Lord of any day! Jesus declared that He was the Lord of the Sabbath which, until the resurrection of Christ, of course, was the seventh day. Since then, it is the first day of the week.

Number ten. He also claimed sinlessness. God alone is holy and sinless. Is there any human being who is sinless? Have not all sinned and come short of the glory of God? There is none righteous, no not one. But Jesus said in John 8:46, "Which of you convicts Me of sin?" Throughout the Bible, those who knew Him best concluded that He was without sin.

He also asserted His pre-existence. He said, "before Abraham was, I AM." He also said, "Your father Abraham rejoiced to see My day, and he saw it and was glad." And the Jews said to Him, "You are not yet fifty years old, and have You seen Abraham?" Jesus said to them, "Most assuredly, I say to you, before Abraham was, I AM" (John 8:56-58).

So, what did the Jews think about that? Did they think, "Well, that's nice"? No, they thought that He was making a claim to deity, that this was blasphemy, and they took up stones to stone Him, which they frequently did because of His claims. He responded, "For which of those works do you stone Me?"

They replied, "For a good work we do not stone You, but for blasphemy, and because You, being a Man, make Yourself God." They understood what He was saying, and they wanted to kill Him for it. He had said that before Abraham was, "I AM."

He asserts also that He is the very manifestation of the Father. In John 14:9, He says, "Have I been with you so long, and yet you have not known Me, Philip? He who has seen Me has seen the Father; so how can you say, 'Show us the Father'?"

What a statement. "If you have seen me, you've seen God." Would you make a claim like that? Of course not. That would be blasphemous. But Jesus declared it, clearly asserting that He was the Son of God. He did so even under oath. Now, we might say "Well, am I not a son of God?" But He never claimed to be *a* son of God, He claimed to be *the* Son of God. In fact, He said that He was the only begotten Son of God.

And listen to this claim from John 5:25: He said, "Most assuredly, I say to you, the hour is coming, and now is, when the dead will hear the voice of the Son of God; and those who hear will live." In Mark 14:61, the High Priest asked Him when He was under oath, "Are You the Christ, the Son of the Blessed?" (i.e., the Son of God). The Jews would usually try to avoid saying the word God.

Jesus said, "I am." Which meant deity, which meant blasphemy, which meant certain death for Christ. Under oath, Jesus said, "I am." That is as clear a claim of deity as you can possibly have. But He did not leave it there. He went on to say, "And you will see the Son of Man sitting at the right hand of the Power."

As we have seen, the Son of Man is a term taken from Daniel, and it was a common term for the Messiah who was to come. "And you will see the Son of Man sitting at the right hand of the Power, and coming with the clouds of heaven." They said to Him that He was committing blasphemy. He did not correct them because He was divine.

Jesus said famously, "For God so loved the world that He gave His only begotten Son, that whoever believes in Him should not perish but have everlasting life." Jesus, very clearly, made the claims of deity. He claimed omniscience, omnipresence, omnipotence. He claimed that He would judge the world, that He would raise the dead, that those who had seen Him had seen the Father, that He was the only begotten Son of God, that He was coming in great power and glory to judge the world, and that He was the very manifestation of the Father. And He made many other such claims.

Yes, Jesus Christ clearly claimed to be divine. There can be no doubt of that. Now, of course, the rest of the Bible makes the claim far more clearly than that. In rising from the dead, He again declared Himself to be the Son of God with power. Like stilling the waves and the winds, when He silently declared His claims of deity, He claims divinity in His resurrection.

Before He was killed, He declared, "No one takes it [My life] from Me, but I lay it down of Myself. I have power to lay it down, and I have power to take it again" (John 10:18). Which of you can say that? That is clearly His preeminent claim to deity. Jesus made that claim without any hesitation, and He proved it with His life.

CONCLUSION

Several other passages proclaim the deity of Christ. Colossians 2:9, for instance, says, "For in Him dwells all the fullness of the Godhead bodily." Jesus was the image of the invisible God. The one divine attribute in the New Testament not attributed to Christ is invisibility. The Father is invisible. Christ is the visible image of the invisible God. Note what the Father says about the Son in Hebrews 1:8. It says in that passage that God says to the angels this and that and the other. "But to the Son He [the Father] says: 'Your throne, O God, is forever.'" The Father talks to the Son and calls him God. Jesus is most clearly the living God. His claims to deity are overwhelming.

CHAPTER 13

More than a Teacher
The Deity of Christ, Part 3

⚜

PROPHECY:

"Your throne, O God, is forever and ever; a scepter of righteousness is the scepter of Your kingdom. You love righteousness and hate wickedness; therefore God, Your God, has anointed You with the oil of gladness more than Your companions."
Psalm 45:6–7

"Of old You laid the foundation of the earth, and the heavens are the work of Your hands. They will perish, but You will endure; yes, they will all grow old like a garment; like a cloak You will change them, and they will be changed. But You are the same, and Your years will have no end."
Psalm 102:25–27

FULFILLMENT:

But to the Son He says: "Your throne, O God, is forever and ever; a scepter of righteousness is the scepter of Your kingdom. You have loved righteousness and hated lawlessness; therefore God, Your God, has anointed You with the oil of gladness more than Your companions."
And: "You, Lord, in the beginning laid the foundation of the earth, and the heavens are the work of Your hands. They will perish, but You

remain; and they will all grow old like a garment; like a cloak You will fold them up, and they will be changed. But You are the same, and Your years will not fail."
Hebrews 1:8–12

These Old Testament prophecies point to the divinity of the Messiah. The coming One was seen as having an eternal throne and being the very Creator of the universe. He was to have absolute power and rule. He was to be morally pure and govern in holiness.

John, the apostle, summarized this vision of the Messiah and applied it to Jesus Christ in the Gospel of John.

> In the beginning was the Word, and the Word was with God, and the Word was God. He was in the beginning with God. All things were made through Him, and without Him nothing was made that was made. In Him was life, and the life was the light of men. And the light shines in the darkness, and the darkness did not comprehend it. ... He was in the world, and the world was made through Him, and the world did not know Him. He came to His own, and His own did not receive Him. But as many as received Him, to them He gave the right to become children of God, to those who believe in His name. ... And the Word became flesh and dwelt among us, and we beheld His glory, the glory as of the only begotten of the Father, full of grace and truth (John 1:1–5, 10–12, 14).

This quote and the Hebrews passage that precedes it indicate that the early Christians truly believed Jesus was the divine Creator

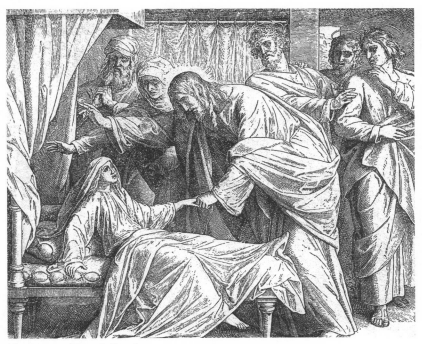

The Raising of Jairus's Daughter

come in the flesh. This is a remarkable testimony since it comes from people who were closely associated with Jesus and knew Him well. Though many would still deny it, the simple fact is that Jesus is the Christ and the Creator of the universe.

CONCLUSION

This is a vital part of our confession. It is not enough to accept Jesus as a great philosopher, moral teacher, religious martyr, or even an angel. We must accept Him as God, the second person of the Trinity. He is 100 percent God and 100 percent man. Unless we accept Him as our Lord and our God, we do not accept Him at all (John 20:27–29).

CHAPTER 14

The Bethlehem Baby

⚜

PROPHECY:
"But you, Bethlehem Ephrathah, though you are little among the thousands of Judah, yet out of you shall come forth to Me the One to be Ruler in Israel, Whose goings forth are from of old, from everlasting."
Micah 5:2

FULFILLMENT:
Joseph also went up from Galilee, out of the city of Nazareth, into Judea, to the city of David, which is called Bethlehem, because he was of the house and lineage of David, to be registered with Mary, his betrothed wife, who was with child. So it was, that while they were there, the days were completed for her to be delivered. And she brought forth her firstborn Son, and wrapped Him in swaddling cloths, and laid Him in a manger, because there was no room for them in the inn.
Luke 2:4–7

Jesus is the Bethlehem Babe. Where He would be born was long foretold by Micah (*circa* 700 B.C.). Imagine accurately foretelling that a ruler would be born in a small town in Mississippi in the year of our Lord 2708. That is roughly what this prophecy is like.

According to *The Zondervan Pictorial Bible Dictionary*, Ephrathah was the "ancient name of Bethlehem or the district around it." Bethlehem was a small town then (we sing even today, "O Little Town of Bethlehem"). It's still a small town, but it was even smaller then. In the catalog of cities given to us by Joshua, and then by Nehemiah—neither one of these even includes Bethlehem. You couldn't even find it on a road map.

Yet 700 years before Christ was born, we are told exactly in which town it will take place. This is not just an ordinary birth. We can talk about the beginning of Caesar, or Alexander the Great, or Napoleon, but Jesus had no beginning. He "shall come forth to Me … Whose goings forth are from of old, from everlasting."

Out of the little town of Bethlehem there was to come forth one who has lived everlastingly, Jesus, the Son of God, the Eternal Second person of the Trinity, was to come forth out of this little town.

BETHLEHEM PREDESTINED CRADLE OF THE WORLD

Skeptics always complain that the prophecies of the Bible are too general and do not deal with concrete occurrences. However, in this case, the prophecy cannot be faulted for clarity. The coming ruler of Israel, whose "goings forth have been from old, from everlasting" shall be born in Bethlehem. He cannot be born in Jerusalem, or Nazareth, or Rome, or Moscow, or Washington. He must be born in the small town of Bethlehem.

As all the world knows, this was, in fact, where Jesus was born. When the wise men from the east arrived in Jerusalem, they inquired where the "King of the Jews" was to be born. Quoting the prophecy in Micah, the biblical scholars of Israel replied that He would be born in Bethlehem. This clarifies that the leaders of Israel knew which town their Messiah had to be from. This is no later Christian interpretation of this passage—but was clearly understood by the Jews at the time of Christ's birth.

What a substantiation of our faith. Our trust in the Bible, God, and Jesus is not built upon fantasies and hopes—but on facts. God

Christ Born in a Bethlehem Stable

can give prophecy and fulfill it because He is the ruler of history. He can not only foresee, but He can also control the events of our world. Therefore, God can bring to pass Christ's entrance into the world, even as He revealed it to Micah in the 8th century B.C. God, unlike all the "gods" and "religions" created by men, is able to accurately prophesy the future.

123

This prophecy in Micah is but one example of the concrete evidence God has given His people to help bolster their faith and assure them of His control over both men and history. The God of the Bible is able to accomplish His promises. That which He has said, He will perform.

Frederich Meldau wrote a booklet on Messianic prophecies in which he states:

> Neither Mary nor Caesar nor the Roman tax collectors did the timing, nor were they in charge of affairs; but the God who rules the world behind the scenes had His hand on the wheel, and He literally "moved the peoples of the world" and timed everything to the very day, so that Mary and Joseph got to Bethlehem in the nick of time, that Jesus, the chosen Messiah, might be born in the right place, the place designated by the infallible finger of prophecy.[43]

Like all of the Messianic prophecies Jesus fulfilled, we see the divine nature of the Bible. Only a God who knows the future could foretell things like this.

CONCLUSION

Faith in Christ is a reasonable faith. It is not some blind emotional high, some empty existential experience, a psychological crutch, or wishful thinking. It is the acceptance of truth and reality. It is rational and realistic to be a Christian, for only in the teachings of the Christian faith can a person find a consistent and rational explanation of the world in which we live.

CHAPTER 15

Rachel Weeping

❦

PROPHECY:

Thus says the Lord: "A voice was heard in Ramah, lamentation and bitter weeping, Rachel weeping for her children, refusing to be comforted for her children, because they are no more."
Jeremiah 31:15

FULFILLMENT:

Then Herod, when he saw that he was deceived by the wise men, was exceedingly angry; and he sent forth and put to death all the male children who were in Bethlehem and in all its districts, from two years old and under, according to the time which he had determined from the wise men. Then was fulfilled what was spoken by Jeremiah the prophet, saying: "A voice was heard in Ramah, lamentation, weeping, and great mourning, Rachel weeping for her children, refusing to be comforted, because they are no more."
Matthew 2:16–18

In Jeremiah, we learn in advance of Herod's tragic slaughter of the innocents. Here is "Rachel weeping" for her children, for they are no more.

Few acts in history have shown the depravity and foolishness of man as clearly as the slaughter of the infants of Bethlehem by Herod the Great, King of Judea. He never doubted the word of the wise men, the priests, or the scribes. He believed, like you and I, that God's appointed King had been born in Bethlehem, but instead of worship, he determined to meet this special child with a sword.

Herod had the audacity to assume that by the use of his military force he could kill God's King and so avoid losing his throne to Christ. Psalm 2:4 describes God as laughing at such vain attempts to stop His sovereign plans. Furthermore, it is important that we recognize that even the sinful acts of men operate within the bounds of God's sovereign will.

Matthew leads us to this principle when he quotes the prophet Jeremiah. Let me explain: When Jeremiah spoke of "Rachel weeping," he was using a poetic mode of expression. Rachel, the wife of Jacob, was the symbolic mother figure of Israel. The prophet used this literary device to convey great national sorrow for the children who were being taken away to captivity in Babylon.

These mothers lost their children, just as the mothers of Bethlehem and the surrounding area lost theirs to a tyrannical king who hoped by his inhuman act to strengthen his political position and prevent an overthrow of his rule. In this historical context, Jeremiah commanded the nation of Israel to dry their tears, for God would bring deliverance from their captors and revive the nation's love for God and His Law.

Matthew finds in this passage a perfect prophecy of the tragic events that follow the worship of Christ by the wise men. The situation is the same. Even as the weeping of the mothers at the time of Jeremiah signified the beginning of a new era of revived spiritual life for Israel, so the weeping of the mothers at the time of Christ signaled the coming deliverance the Messiah would bring (Jeremiah

126

The Massacre of the Innocents

31:7). Matthew proclaims that Jeremiah's prophecy was "fulfilled," because the same spiritual principle of "sorrow preceding salvation" was operating in the first century.

Who are the "Herods" of our age? Where are the political leaders who would dare use military strength to stop God's Messiah? They are found in the remnant Communist countries which persecute Christians, in the nations dominated by Islam which prohibit the free proclamation of the Gospel, and in other tyrannical governments around the world which hinder Christians from sharing their faith. An estimated 200 million believers live in lands where Christianity is persecuted. The blood of Christian martyrs flows around the world because men vainly believe they can use physical force to prevent God from accomplishing His plan. The infants of Bethlehem have often been viewed historically by the Church as the first Christian martyrs.

No force in heaven or earth can stop God's plan. Christ's Church and Christ's Kingdom shall prosper until they encompass the entire earth. To resist the King of kings is foolish, for no man or nation can stop the purpose of God.

CONCLUSION

Though the present time may be filled with sorrow, do not despair, for the God of deliverance still hears the prayers of His people and is able and willing to bring His hand of deliverance and salvation into your life.

CHAPTER 16

Daniel's Seventy Weeks

ॐ

PROPHECY:

"Know therefore and understand, that from the going forth of the command to restore and build Jerusalem until Messiah the Prince, there shall be seven weeks and sixty-two weeks; the street shall be built again, and the wall, even in troublesome times."
Daniel 9:25

"Seventy weeks are determined for your people and for your holy city, to finish the transgression, to make an end of sins, to make reconciliation for iniquity, to bring in everlasting righteousness, to seal up vision and prophecy, and to anoint the Most Holy. … And after the sixty-two weeks Messiah shall be cut off, but not for Himself; and the people of the prince who is to come shall destroy the city and the sanctuary. The end of it shall be with a flood, and till the end of the war desolations are determined."
Daniel 9:24, 26

FULFILLMENT:

But when the fullness of the time had come, God sent forth His Son, born of a woman, born under the law…
Galatians 4:4

The prophecy of the seventy weeks of Daniel is perhaps the most brilliant in all of Scripture. Liberals and skeptics have no answer for the clear and precise prophecy by Daniel as to when the promised Messiah would come. Without supernatural revelation, no mere man could have set forth the intricate prophetic view recorded in the ninth chapter of Daniel.

In this prophecy, it is promised that "[s]eventy weeks are determined for your people and for your holy city, to finish the transgression, to make an end of sins, to make reconciliation for iniquity, to bring in everlasting righteousness, to seal up vision and prophecy, and to anoint the Most Holy" (v. 24). God predestined that in the time span of "seventy weeks," six results would be accomplished:

- First, it is promised that God would "finish the transgression." This speaks of a final redemptive act, which will satisfy God's righteousness. Within this specific period of time, God will move in a mighty way to redeem and forgive His people.
- Second, God promised to "make an end of sins." The power of sin and death will be broken. No longer would sin rule men, but the tyranny of sin would be cast off.
- Third, God proclaimed that He would "make reconciliation for iniquity." A final and everlasting atonement would be made. The legal charges against God's people would be dropped because they had been paid for by a sacrifice. There would be complete reconciliation between God and His people.
- Fourth, this redemptive act of God would not just cover and forgive sin, but would actually bring in "everlasting righteousness." God's people would be accounted righteous again in His sight.
- Fifth, the Old Testament prophecies would be totally fulfilled in the "seventy weeks," and all they had foretold would come to pass. The prophecy and the vision of the Old Testament era would be "sealed."

- Sixth and finally, God would "anoint the Most Holy," or translated literally, "anoint a holiness of holinesses." This speaks of God pouring out His Spirit upon the Messiah. The Messiah will have the Spirit without measure and be the anointed Prophet, Priest, and King of God.

All six of these objectives are Messianic in their character and speak of God fulfilling His redemptive promises to His people. Daniel must have been overwhelmed with the greatness of this revelation, for he now would understand when God's promises would be completed.

For us to appreciate this prophecy's accuracy, we must carefully study the passage itself, the symbolic use of language in Hebrew literature, and the history of the ancient world. To begin with, it is necessary for us to understand that each day of these weeks represents one year. Therefore, 70 weeks represent 490 years (7 "days" x 70 "weeks" = 490 years).

Why should we understand these "weeks" as years and not days? First of all, it would be irrational to think the entire city, including the temple and perimeter wall could be built in 490 days. This was simply a physical impossibility at the time. Second, history records the restoration of the city under the leadership of Ezra and Nehemiah during the 5th century B.C. If we understand these "weeks" as having days that equal a year, the first part of the prophecy, speaking of the restoration of the city, is fulfilled on schedule. When this is combined with the symbolic nature of prophetic literature, it is not unreasonable for us to assume that these "days" are, in fact, years.

The "seventy weeks" that Daniel refers to are broken up into three different categories.

1. Seven weeks or 49 years will elapse from the decree to rebuild the Holy City until the wall of Jerusalem would actually be restored. This was accomplished under the leadership of Ezra and Nehemiah.

2. Following this first phase, 62 more weeks—434 years—

The Prophet Daniel

will pass until the appearance and anointing of "Messiah the Prince."

3. During the last phase of this prophecy, which Daniel indicates is one week, or seven years in duration, the Messiah will be "cut off, but not for himself."

We can see from this that it should be possible to calculate the time when the Old Testament predicted the Messiah would appear and accomplish His work. The only historical fact needed is the date of the "decree to restore and rebuild Jerusalem."

There are four decrees that could be interpreted as the *terminus a quo*, or starting date, for this prophecy. They are:

1. Cyrus' decree in Ezra 1:1–4, dated 539 B.C.
2. Darius' decree in Ezra 5:3–7, dated 519 B.C.
3. Artaxerxes' decree in Ezra 7:11–16, dated 458 B.C.
4. Artaxerxes' decree in Nehemiah 2:1–8, dated 445 B.C.

One of these four dates must serve as the beginning date of the prophecy in Daniel. Theologians have historically accepted three different views of this prophecy, each employing a different date as the proper *terminus a quo.*

1. Liberal scholars, who do not believe in the complete trustworthiness of Scripture and doubt the supernatural nature of biblical prophecy, interpret this passage as speaking of Antiochus Epiphanes, a political ruler symbolically referred to in other prophecies by Daniel.

Antiochus Epiphanes—a blaspheming, decadent, Greek ruler—hardly *fulfills* the Messianic promises found in this passage. Even if we accept him as the *fulfillment* of this prophecy, the early date of 539 B.C., to which the liberal scholars hold, makes the prophecy accurate only within a few decades of Epiphanes' career.

2. The second theory, popular among Bible-believing theologians, is held by many in the Church today. It is based on the dispensational theory and includes a huge gap between the 69th and the 70th week. The last week of Daniel's "seventy weeks" is translated as still future and is perceived as "the great tribulation."

Because this view usually accepts the date of 445 B.C. as the beginning of the prophecy of the seventy weeks, it is forced to place Christ's death at 33 A.D. However, there is some historical evidence to argue that Christ died in 30 A.D.

It also seems to be a very artificial and arbitrary understanding of the text to place 2,000 years (or more) between the 69th and 70th week. It is hard to understand how such an interpretation could be the intended meaning of this prophecy.

3. The traditional view accepts the first decree by Artaxerxes in 458 B.C. as the correct starting point for this prophecy. The reason for this is that the decrees by Cyrus and Darius deal only with rebuilding the temple, but Artaxerxes' decree concerns the reconstruction of the city. When one calculates the prophecy from this time, we find that the 69 weeks end in 26 A.D., with the Messiah being "cut off" in 30 A.D.

The traditional view which places the appearing of the Messiah at 26 A.D. would seem to be the most rational and clear understanding of the Old Testament passage.

It is noteworthy, therefore, that it places the appearing of the promised Savior and King of the Jews at the same time as the baptism of Jesus. How do I know this? Luke makes it very clear that Jesus was baptized by John and publicly proclaimed to be the promised Messiah in the "fifteenth year of the reign of Tiberius Caesar" (Luke 3:1). Tiberius Caesar began his rule in 11 A.D., and therefore, the fifteenth year of his reign would be 26 A.D.

This, therefore, clearly dates the baptism of Christ and His anointing by the Holy Spirit at the same time as the fulfillment of Daniel's prophecy. It also places Christ's death on the Cross in 30 A.D., the very time when Daniel prophesied that the Messiah would be "cut off, but not for himself."

This shows beyond a shadow of a doubt that Jesus of Nazareth was, in fact, the promised Messiah of the Jews and the Redeemer of His people. Through His death on the Cross and His resurrection from the grave, He paid for transgression, ended the power of sin, made reconciliation for iniquity, brought in everlasting righteousness, fulfilled the prophecies of the Old Testament, and was the anointed Holy One.

Please note that Bible-believing scholars can be found who believe that Jesus died in 30 A.D., as well as equal scholars who believe He died in 33 A.D. If the 30 year figure is correct, then the first Good Friday was April 7 and Easter was April 9. (These dates are based on the Friday on which Passover fell.) If the later year is correct, then Good Friday was April 3, 33, and Easter Sunday, April 5, 33. It does not matter that we cannot know for sure which of these two dates for the crucifixion is correct—what does matter is that Jesus died for our sins and rose again from the dead, changing all of history.

CONCLUSION

Every person who reads and believes the Old Testament should recognize Jesus as the true Messiah. Clearly, He fulfilled the prophecy of Daniel exactly as God prophesied hundreds of years before. Christianity is a faith built upon the clear evidence that God is working in history through Jesus Christ.

CHAPTER 17

A Prophetic Parallel

❦

PROPHECY:
"When Israel was a child, I loved him, and out of Egypt I called My son."
Hosea 11:1

FULFILLMENT:
When he arose, he took the young Child and His mother by night and departed for Egypt, and was there until the death of Herod, that it might be fulfilled which was spoken by the Lord through the prophet, saying, "Out of Egypt I called My Son."
Matthew 2:14–15

If we read the Old Testament prophecies in their historical context, we can see that some of them are very clearly prophecies of Jesus and their fulfillment is easily understood. However, others seem like vague references, which are taken out of context when perceived as Messianic in character. How can we explain such prophecies, and why did the writers of the New Testament believe these passages spoke of Christ?

For the New Testament writers, Jesus Christ was the fulfillment

The Flight Into Egypt

of the Old Testament prophecies, and His life revealed the true meaning behind the panorama of Israel's history and people (Colossians 2:17). They firmly believed that God controlled the events of Christ's life so that every "jot and tittle" of Scripture would come to pass.

So it is that Matthew applies this passage in Hosea 11 to Christ, which in its historical context speaks of Israel's deliverance from Egypt. Yet, because Matthew deeply understood the purpose and nature of Jesus' ministry, he sees here an amazing parallel between the life of Christ and the historical life of the nation of Israel.

Matthew recounts how the young Jesus was taken to Egypt to escape Herod's murderous intentions and then returned with His parents after Herod died. For Matthew, this is no mere historical incident but, inspired by the Holy Spirit, he perceives that the great deliverance Hosea speaks of was a foreshadowing of Christ's return from Egypt with His parents.

Matthew uses this Old Testament passage to refer to Jesus, for he realizes that this small child is the "New Israel" from which shall come the true redemptive community. Jesus would go through water at His baptism and then sojourn in the desert as He followed the leading of God, even as the nation of Israel followed God through the Red Sea and into the wilderness under the leadership of Moses (Matthew 3:13–4:11). As Israel had twelve tribes, so Christ would choose twelve apostles who would be the spiritual fathers of the new "spiritual Israel," whose Godgiven destiny is to fulfill the Abrahamic promise that God's chosen people would inherit the whole earth (Romans 4:13).

CONCLUSION

As we study the Old Testament Scripture, we should, like Matthew, use the life of Christ as a light to read by. For everything in the Old Testament was written to teach us to have hope in Jesus Christ (Romans 15:4). Therefore, we must strive to understand the Old Testament from a "Christological" perspective and not merely as an obscure history of an ancient civilization. Israel was the chosen vessel from which Christ was to come, and all of its history gives testimony to His ministry, person, and word. Study of the Old Testament, then, is vital for the maturing of our faith and our understanding of Jesus Christ.

CHAPTER 18

Mysteries of the Kingdom

❧

PROPHECY:

*I will open my mouth in a parable; I will utter dark sayings of old,
which we have heard and known, and our fathers have told us. We
will not hide them from their children, telling to the generation to come
the praises of the Lord, and His strength and His wonderful works
that He has done.*
Psalm 78:2–4

FULFILLMENT:

*All these things Jesus spoke to the multitude in parables; and without
a parable He did not speak to them, that it might be fulfilled which
was spoken by the prophet, saying: "I will open My mouth in parables;
I will utter things kept secret from the foundation of the world."*
Matthew 13:34–35

In the history of all of the world's teachers, there has never
been anyone who used the parable as skillfully and brilliantly as Jesus
Christ. He was the parable teacher *par excellence*.

The Old Testament promised that God would speak in parables
and reveal things never known before. In fulfillment of this

prophecy, Jesus used the parable as one of the major techniques in His teaching ministry.

It is important for us to note that through parables Christ revealed a new dimension of God's purpose and plan. While based upon and in accord with Old Testament revelation, Christ's parables brought into the full light of day God's strategy for the redemption of His creation (Matthew 13:52).

Christ was the wisdom of God personified. He taught Israel through the parable of the sower that the Kingdom of God would be planted in the hearts of men through the teaching of the Gospel before its social impact would be felt (Matthew 13:3–9). Jesus also pointed out in the parable of the net and the parable of the tares that, until the final judgment, the Kingdom would be a mixture of both believers and unbelievers (Matthew 13:24–29; 47–50). The parable of the mustard seed taught that the Kingdom would increase in influence and size, beginning as a small seed and growing into the greatest tree in all the earth (Matthew 13:31–32).

These teachings radically contradicted the Jewish concept of the Kingdom of God—which they thought would come suddenly through a cataclysmic war led by God's Messiah against the Gentile nations. Instead, Jesus emphasized that, prior to the day of judgment, God's rule or Kingdom would enter through the ministry of the Son of Man and the teaching of the apostles, creating spiritual life in the hearts of men, regardless of nationality.

The people of the Kingdom would not be chosen by natural descent from Abraham—but only by faith in Jesus Christ and the Gospel. Through the teaching of the Word, this Kingdom would fill the earth (Matthew 13). God's Messiah would conquer through conversion before He judged His enemies in wrath (Isaiah 2:1–6).

CONCLUSION

These revelations, and many others, were taught by Christ through parables. All that He foretold would come to be: The Gospel would be preached first to the Jews, then to the Samaritans, and finally to the Gentiles. The Christian Gospel has filled the earth, and every day, thousands of people turn to Christ and accept Him as their Lord and Savior. Christ's conquest goes on, hour by hour, day by day, ever increasing the size and power of His Kingdom. It is our privilege as Christians to be His Kingdom people and commit ourselves to the expanding rule of Christ into every area of our private and public lives. Christ's Kingdom confronts each of us with the responsibility of responding to His gracious call to be Kingdom builders.

CHAPTER 19

No Chariots

❧

PROPHECY:

Rejoice greatly, O daughter of Zion! Shout, O daughter of Jerusalem!
Behold, your King is coming to you; He is just and having salvation,
lowly and riding on a donkey, a colt, the foal of a donkey.
Zechariah 9:9

FULFILLMENT:

Then they brought the colt to Jesus and threw their clothes on it, and
He sat on it.... Then those who went before and those who followed
cried out, saying: "Hosanna! Blessed is He who comes in the name of
the Lord!" ... And Jesus went into Jerusalem....
Mark 11:7, 9, 11

Hundreds of years before Christ entered the city of Jerusalem, Zechariah envisioned that the Messiah would enter riding upon the foal of a donkey. The picture here is that the Messiah would come, not as a great military general, not as a mighty conqueror on a warhorse, but as a ruler who would reign with humility and peace.

Christ purposely fulfilled this vision of the coming Messiah. The people understood the symbolism Jesus was using and responded

Entry of Jesus Into Jerusalem

in joyful acceptance. By this action, He clearly identified Himself with the Messianic image that Zechariah painted, communicating to all Israel His claim to the Messianic role.

FIRST COMING IN GRACE

The first coming of Christ was characterized by a demonstration of God's patience, mercy, and grace. Christ came as the healer, counselor, and teacher (Isaiah 61:1–6).

Excited by His ministry and the fact that He had raised Lazarus from the dead several days before, the people were ready to accept Jesus as the long awaited Messiah. However, once He was arrested and the Jewish leaders publicly declared their intention to punish Him for blasphemy, the people mistook His patience and mercy for weakness and turned against Him. They simply failed to understand the purpose and plan of God's redemption.

God's intention was for His chosen Messiah to pay for the sins of God's people, be raised and ascended to glory, and leave a group of disciples upon the earth who would spread His message. All this Jesus accomplished (John 17:1–5). Christ won the victory at the Cross, which in principle destroyed the works of the devil and crippled the power of sin (Colossians 2:8–15). Christ now sits at God the Father's right hand, ruling over the nations. His enemies are slowly but surely being conquered by the spread of the Gospel.

Jesus understood the intention of the Father. He taught that His first ministry would be one of mercy and humility and that He would return again in power and glory (Luke 19:12–28).

Many in historic Judaism have claimed that Jesus cannot be the Jewish Messiah, since He failed to usher in world peace through military conquest. As we have seen, this position fails to do justice to the Old Testament view of the Messiah and Jesus' own revelation of the Messianic mission.

CONCLUSION

As Christians, we need to have a firm grasp of the New Testament's revelation regarding the first coming of Christ. We must clearly proclaim that Christ's ministry was a total success and in agreement with God's decree (John 18:34-37; 19:11). Just as Jesus purposely fulfilled the prophecy of His entry into Jerusalem, He will fulfill His promised Second Coming. We should be anxiously awaiting that event when the full manifestation of His power and glory will be made known to all mankind.

CHAPTER 20

The Faith of a Child

⚜

PROPHECY:

From the lips of children and infants you have ordained praise because of your enemies, to silence the foe and the avenger.
Psalm 8:2 NIV

FULFILLMENT:

But when the chief priests and scribes saw the wonderful things that He did, and the children crying out in the temple and saying, "Hosanna to the Son of David!" they were indignant and said to Him, "Do You hear what these are saying?" And Jesus said to them, "Yes. Have you never read, 'Out of the mouth of babes and nursing infants You have perfected praise'?"
Matthew 21:15–16

When the young children of Jerusalem joined the crowd at the temple and proclaimed Jesus as the Messiah, the "son of David," they fulfilled the Old Testament promise that "babes" would give praise to God. The religious leaders were outraged at this outburst of faith from mere "children" and demanded they be silenced. Yet, Jesus knew that these words had been placed in the mouths of these chil-

Jesus Blessing the Little Children

dren by God.

Jesus viewed all children with a special love. He said, "Let the little children come to Me, and do not forbid them; for of such is the kingdom of heaven" (Matthew 19:14). It is interesting to note that, according to biblical scholar Oscar Cullmann, these words, in all probability, were used as a formal liturgical formula for baptism of children in the early church.

This underscores the position that the children of believers should be baptized into the covenant, just as the male children of Israel were circumcised into the Abrahamic covenant in the Old Testament (Genesis 17:12–13). Baptism replaces circumcision as the sign of the Abrahamic covenant, now that Christ has come and fulfilled all the promises given to Abraham (Colossians 2:11–12; Romans 4; Acts 2:39). These "covenant children" are separated for a special ministry of the Spirit and should be taught by the Christian community the full counsel of God's Word, both in word and in practice (Deuteronomy 6:7–9; 1 Corinthians 7:14). The children will be held responsible for this greater revelation of God's grace because they have a greater opportunity to respond in faith.

It is vital, as Christian parents and as communities of believers, that we dedicate ourselves to the godly rearing of our children, re-membering the fearful warning of Christ concerning those who would "offend" these little ones (Matthew 18:6). Each of us must do all we can to minister to our own children and raise them in the fear of the Lord. We must insist on having ministries within the local church that help young people to trust in Christ as their personal Lord and Savior.

Jesus loved the little children and they loved Him. They pro-claimed His praises throughout the streets of Jerusalem. As God had planned, His chosen Messiah would be received by the humble chil-dren who could see in Jesus their Savior (Matthew 18:3–4).

CONCLUSION

We must become like little children in order to enter God's Kingdom (Matthew 18:1–4). Just as children depend on others to live, we must learn to depend on God and His salvation through Christ in order to be saved. Just as a child trusts his parents for phys-ical and emotional needs, so we must learn to trust in Christ Jesus. The humility and simplicity of a child's trust is what Jesus is looking for in us. As a child trusts his parents to know best, so we must trust His goodness and His power to lead us safely home.

CHAPTER 21

Trouble in the Temple

❦

PROPHECY:
"Behold, I send My messenger, and he will prepare the way before Me. And the Lord, whom you seek, will suddenly come to His temple, even the Messenger of the covenant, in whom you delight. Behold, He is coming," says the Lord of hosts.
Malachi 3:1

Because zeal for Your house has eaten me up, and the reproaches of those who reproach You have fallen on me.
Psalm 69:9

FULFILLMENT:
Now the Passover of the Jews was at hand, and Jesus went up to Jerusalem. And He found in the temple those who sold oxen and sheep and doves, and the moneychangers doing business. When He had made a whip of cords, He drove them all out of the temple, with the sheep and the oxen, and poured out the changers' money and overturned the tables. And He said to those who sold doves, "Take these things away! Do not make My Father's house a house of merchandise!" Then His disciples remembered that it was written, "Zeal for Your house has eaten Me up."
John 2:13–17

Jesus Christ had a forerunner. In Malachi (the last book of the Hebrew Bible), we learn of John the Baptist, the new Elijah, who comes to prepare the way for the Lord. We also learn that Messiah will come to the temple and shake things up.

THE HOLY COURTS OF GOD?

If you knew that Jesus was going to worship in your church this Sunday, would it affect your attitude or the way you participated in the service? Would there be any part of the order of worship you would want to leave out?

Malachi prophesied that the day would come when "the Lord" would appear in His temple and examine the worship of His people on a firsthand basis. Jesus Christ fulfilled this promise when He went to the temple in Jerusalem and cleansed it, casting out those who were exploiting the worship of God for personal economic gain.

The Scriptures teach that Jesus was motivated by a holy zeal for the honor of the God of Israel and for God's house. He was distressed that the place of prayer had become a means of profit. Rising up in holy anger, He evicted those who dared to pollute the holy courts of God's temple with their crass materialism. He actually put Himself in physical danger because of His burning desire that the worship of God be kept both pure and holy.

By His example, Christ Jesus teaches us that it is vital that we do God's work in God's way. God cannot be honored by our disobedient, hypocritical, and halfhearted worship (Numbers 3:4). In both the Old and New Testaments, God condemns unbiblical methods of worship, the exploitation of religion for economic gain, and the "public" offering of money to garner man's praise (2 Corinthians 4:1–5; Leviticus 10:1–3; Acts 5:1–11; Matthew 6:1–4).

Today, God's temple is the Church (Ephesians 2:20–22). Christ demands that our worship conform to the express will of God, as revealed in His Word, and in a spirit of godly fear and sincerity.

While it is proper for God's people to support God's work with their tithes and offerings, it is wrong when religious leaders attempt

Jesus Clearing the Temple

to gain personal wealth and prestige through their ministry (Acts 4:37; Acts 8:17–20; 1 Peter 5:1–3). Sometimes pastors go beyond Scripture, trying to make people feel guilty for not doing enough or giving enough. The Gospel should never be used for gain.

CONCLUSION

God yearns for true worship from His people, in spirit and in truth (John 4:24). As we gather together in our local churches this week, let us remember the importance of worshiping God by the standard of His Word and in an attitude of godly fear (Ecclesiastes 5:1–2).

I suppose a skeptic could argue that this prophecy that Jesus fulfilled when He cleansed the temple was one that He could have set out to fulfill. Thus, there would be no miraculous element to it. But how in the world could He have fulfilled what happened to Him on Good Friday, as we will see in the next couple of chapters? And why would He wish that upon Himself, unless He truly was the Messiah?

CHAPTER 22

A Familiar Friend

❂

PROPHECY:

*Even my own familiar friend in whom I trusted, who ate my bread,
has lifted up his heel against me.*
Psalm 41:9

FULFILLMENT:

*"I [Jesus] do not speak concerning all of you. I know whom I have cho-
sen; but that the Scripture may be fulfilled, 'He who eats bread with
Me has lifted up his heel against Me.'"*
John 13:18

The betrayal of Jesus Christ by Judas Iscariot has inflamed the minds of men throughout history. To this day, Judas' name remains a synonym for "traitor." Judas, who had been one of the twelve apostles, specially chosen as a companion and friend by Jesus Christ, turned against the Son of God because of greed and a lack of true faith (John 12:6).

Judas is the archetype of those who claim to have faith—and are even involved in Christian service—but whose hearts have never been fully won over to the Lord. Such men may preach great ser-

The Judas Kiss

mons and do great deeds, yet they lack any personal and saving knowledge of Jesus Christ (Matthew 7:21–23).

Such people serve Christ while it meets their emotional, economic, and social needs, but when tribulation or persecution arises, these "believers" turn against Him (Matthew 13:20–21). Sometimes it is not persecution but merely a love for riches and the affairs of the world system that cause these people to openly denounce Christ after professing Him as their Lord (Matthew 13:22).

It is important for us to recognize that such people *never had* true saving faith, but merely an outward profession of commitment. They were, in fact, never saved; they simply appeared to be believers. God always knew their hearts and always knew that in reality they had not yet repented and believed in Jesus Christ. They went out from among us because they never really belonged to us.

However, we are incapable of discerning the true nature of a person's faith. Therefore, it is necessary for us to accept the profession of men as sincere. Scripture teaches that it is improper for us to judge the hearts of others. God alone knows our heart, and He alone will be our final judge (1 Kings 8:39).

As Christians, though, we must be aware that there will be those who turn against the faith and renounce their professed Christian beliefs. Each generation will have "disciples" who will publicly appear to be great men of God and then betray this trust. Some will be religious con men, using people in order to become rich (Jude 11; Acts 8:18–20). Others will simply give in under the pressures of public persecution or social pressure because they never were reborn into the family of God.

When we see such men commit apostasy, we must not allow it to weaken our faith. We must clearly understand that God knows those who belong to His Kingdom and loses none of them, yet He demands that all those who call on Jesus as Savior and Lord depart from the practice of evil (2 Timothy 2:19). To deny Christ is a great sin, so let us each day reaffirm our faith and commitment to Christ. True faith is an enduring faith that does not quit when circumstances become difficult.

CONCLUSION

It is a tragic fact of the passion of our Lord Jesus that He was betrayed by a close associate. Judas Iscariot chose the love of money over the love of God and thus betrayed His master, not realizing that he was fulfilling prophecy in the process. Chapter 23 will discuss this betrayal more thoroughly, in particular the price involved and what happened to that money.

CHAPTER 23

The Sacrificial Lamb

❦

PROPHECY:

If he offers a lamb as his offering, then he shall offer it before the Lord.
And he shall lay his hand on the head of his offering, and kill it before
the tabernacle of meeting; and Aaron's sons shall sprinkle its blood all
around on the altar.
Leviticus 3:7-8

FULFILLMENT:

The next day John saw Jesus coming toward him, and said, "Behold!
The Lamb of God who takes away the sin of the world!"
John 1:29

In passage after passage of Exodus, Leviticus, and Numbers, there are detailed descriptions of the animal sacrifices proscribed by God for the purpose of the forgiveness of sins. All of these foreshadow the once-and-for-all sacrifice of Jesus for our sins. Jesus is the ultimate sacrificial lamb. He is the Lamb of God who takes away the sin of the world. He is without blemish. He is both the scapegoat for our transgressions and the one sacrificed for the same. We see the Messianic prophecies about Jesus dying for our sins culminating in Psalm 22. (Isaiah 53 also deals with this at length, and Part III of this book examines that passage, as well.)

Here is a typical statement from the Pentateuch (the first five books of the Bible), from Moses' law on animal sacrifices for forgiveness of sins (again, all of which pointed to Jesus' death on the Cross):

> This is the ordinance of the law which the Lord has commanded, saying: "Speak to the children of Israel, that they bring you a red heifer without blemish, in which there is no defect and on which a yoke has never come. You shall give it to Eleazar the priest, that he may take it outside the camp, and it shall be slaughtered before him" (Numbers 19:2-3).

All of these sacrifices foreshadowed Jesus' sacrifice. The writer of Hebrews said this to some early professing Christians, who were apparently trying to return to Temple Judaism: "For it is impossible for the blood of bulls and goats to take away sins.... [W]e have been sanctified through the offering of the body of Jesus Christ once for all (Hebrews 10:4, 10, ESV).

THE CENTRAL FACT OF THE NEW TESTAMENT

So not only do we find a few hundred specific prophecies about the coming Messiah in the Old Testament that Jesus fulfilled (a portion of which comprise all the chapters in Parts II and III of this book), but we also see that the *entire* sacrificial system with its myriad of regulations pointed to Him.

The central fact of the New Testament is the Cross of Jesus Christ. It is the central fact of Christianity. It is the hope of mankind, where the incarnate God suffered and paid for all of our transgressions. Interestingly and properly, it is the central fact of Old Testament prophecy, as well. Every minute detail of the sufferings of Jesus Christ is described in the Old Testament.

"All those who see Me ridicule Me; they shoot out
the lip, they shake the head, saying, 'He trusted in
the Lord, let Him rescue Him; let Him deliver Him,
since He delights in Him!'" (Psalm 22:7-8).

This is exactly, of course, what the High Priest said as he stood
around Christ. What did they give Him to drink? A thousand years
before His birth the psalmist prophesied: "They also gave me gall
for my food, and for my thirst they gave me vinegar to drink" (Psalm
69:21). So they offered Him vinegar with gall to drink. He suffered
vicariously, substitutionarily, for the sins of others.

We know that the apostles scattered when Jesus was arrested.
Meanwhile, the prophet Zechariah had written centuries before:

"...Strike the Shepherd, and the sheep will be
scattered; then I will turn My hand against the little
ones" (Zechariah 13:7) ...

... and they did that.

He was sold by Judas for 30 pieces of silver. And almost 500
years before that, Zechariah the prophet said,

"If it is agreeable to you, give me my wages....
So they weighed out for my wages thirty pieces of
silver" (Zechariah 11:12).

Do you remember what happened to that silver? Judas relented,
came back, told the priests he had betrayed innocent blood, and
they said to him, "What is that to us? You see to it!" (Matthew 27:4).
And he took the 30 pieces of silver and threw them down in the
temple. They took the silver and bought a potter's field for the burial
of the indigent. Yet 500 years before that, the prophet Zechariah
said,

"'Throw it to the potter'—that princely price they
set on me. So I took the thirty pieces of silver and
threw them into the house of the Lord for the potter" (Zechariah 11:13).

Jesus Falling Beneath the Cross

All this happened to Christ, but it was prophesied hundreds of years before.

"They pierced My hands and My feet," said the prophet David 1,000 years before Christ was born, and 400 years before crucifixion was invented (Psalm 22:16). The hands and feet of David were never pierced, but he spoke as a prophet of that One who was to come.

Crucifixion was invented in 600 B.C. by the Phoenicians. It was adopted by the Romans around 200 B.C. Eight hundred years before the Romans ever heard of crucifixion, David prophesied the piercing of hands and feet (Psalm 22:16).

PSALM 22

For Christians, there is no doubt that Psalm 22 depicts Jesus Christ's experience at Calvary. It graphically describes the physical and emotional trauma that Jesus suffered on the Cross. This Psalm was considered by Jewish scholars to be a Messianic psalm long before Christ came, according to Knox Theological Seminary professor, Sam Lamerson.[44] Only an inspired Word would be able to prophesy all the things contained herein. Here are major portions of that Psalm:

> [1]My God, My God, why have You forsaken Me? …
> [6]But I am a worm, and no man;
> A reproach of men, and despised by the people.
> [7]All those who see Me ridicule Me;
> They shoot out the lip, they shake the head, saying,
> [8]"He trusted in the LORD, let Him rescue Him;
> Let Him deliver Him, since He delights in Him."…
> [12]Many bulls have surrounded Me;
> Strong bulls of Bashan have encircled Me.
> [13]They gape at Me with their mouths,
> Like a raging and roaring lion.
> [14]I am poured out like water,
> And all My bones are out of joint;
> My heart is like wax;
> It has melted within Me.
> [15]My strength is dried up like a potsherd,
> And My tongue clings to My jaws;
> You have brought Me to the dust of death.
> [16]For dogs have surrounded Me;
> The congregation of the wicked has enclosed Me.

They pierced My hands and My feet;
¹⁷I can count all My bones.
They look and stare at Me.
¹⁸They divide My garments among them,
And for My clothing they cast lots....
²²I will declare Your name to My brethren;
In the midst of the assembly I will praise You....
²⁷All the ends of the world
Shall remember and turn to the LORD,
And all the families of the nations
Shall worship before You.
²⁸For the kingdom is the LORD's,
And He rules over the nations.

The painful details of Christ's death are contained in this prophecy. The Psalm foretells of His mockery (v. 8), shame (vv. 13, 17), the pain of crucifixion (vv. 14-16), and the parting of His garments (v. 18). All of these details were controlled and enacted by people who were only interested in ending the life of a "troublemaker." The Psalm provides more convincing evidence of the divine origin of the Scriptures and the faithfulness of God to His Word.

Psalm 22 cries out from the Old Testament for a greater fulfillment than the suffering of any of the Old Testament kings. David could never have imagined that his suffering would lead to such significant results. Only the suffering and resurrection of Jesus Christ could have had such universal consequences, as are foretold in the latter part of this prophetic Psalm (vv. 22-31). In this Old Testament account of Calvary, we have before us a moving prophecy of the Messiah's suffering.

AFTER HIS DEATH

After Jesus died, when they came to break His bones, as they broke the legs of the two on the other crosses, they saw that He was already dead, so they did not break His legs. They pierced His side, however, to make certain. Moses said, more than 1,400 years before:

- "Nor shall you break one of its [the Passover Lamb's] bones" (Exodus 12:46).
- "He guards all his bones; not one of them is broken" (Psalm 34:20).

Was the piercing of His side revealed? "[T]hey will look on Me whom they pierced" (Zechariah 12:10).

He was buried in the grave of Joseph of Arimathaea, a rich man. Isaiah had said some 700 years before, "And he made his grave with the rich in his death" (Isaiah 53:9). Jesus saw not corruption, felt not the gnawing worm, but was raised incorruptible from the dead.

Not only did He rise from the dead, but we know from the psalmist that He ascended into Heaven: "You have ascended on high, You have led captivity captive; You have received gifts among men" (Psalm 68:18).

And the greatest of those gifts is the gift of eternal life, which Christ came into the world to give to all of those who would receive Him and trust in Him. He is the High Priest forever. He is the chief cornerstone of His Church, and

- "... the Gentiles shall seek Him, and His resting place shall be glorious" (Isaiah 11:10).
- "The Lord said to my Lord, 'Sit at My right hand'" (Psalm 110:1). This is God's grand plan, and it is in the process of being fulfilled even now.
- "[W]hen He had by Himself purged our sins, sat down at the right hand of the Majesty on high" (Hebrews 1:3).

CONCLUSION

The Bible can be condensed into the sacrifice of Jesus Christ. When John the Baptist saw Jesus, he said, "Behold! The Lamb of God who takes away the sin of the world!" (John 1:29). Here is a summary of the whole message of the Bible. Jesus Christ, the perfect Son of God and Son of Man, lived a perfect life and died in our place so that those who believe in Him may receive salvation.

CHAPTER 24

The Passover Lamb

PROPHECY:
*"Then they are to take some of the blood and put it on the sides and
tops of the doorframes of the houses where they eat the lambs."*
Exodus 12:7 NIV

FULFILLMENT:
For indeed Christ, our Passover, was sacrificed for us.
1 Corinthians 5:7

The story of the first Passover in Exodus 12 tells, in a nutshell,
the story of Christ's sacrifice. Only when we are covered by "the
blood of the Lamb" are we safe from the wrath of God. Only then
does the wrath of God pass over us.

THE NIGHT OF RETRIBUTION

"And it came to pass at midnight that the LORD struck all the
firstborn in the land of Egypt" (Exodus 12:29). What a momentous
night that was, indeed. In fact, other than that glorious night when
the brightness of heaven broke into the gloom of night and that
angel chorus sang, "Glory to God in the highest," and that other

night at noon, when the darkness of Hell crept in upon the brightness of day, and the Son of God gave forth His life upon the Cross— this night, the last night of Israel in Egypt, was the most momentous night in the history of the world. On that night the entire course of history was turned.

When the sun sank that night on Egypt, Israel was but a horde of slaves and captives galling in their chains, miserable and dejected. But when the morning sun broke that next day, they were a nation on the march—a nation sprung full blown from the heart and mind of God. What a glorious day that was.

But first, there was the night of retribution. Bible commentator Clarence Macartney describes that night so well. The following passage includes a paraphrase of some of his descriptions of the original Passover.

> Over all Egypt it is night. The April moon sheds its golden light over all the land. Against the clear sky rises the mighty Pyramid of Cheops, and in front of that pyramid the Sphinx stares out over the white moonlit desert with stony, mysterious, inscrutable gaze. By the banks of the winding Nile and the numerous canals, tall palm trees wave their branches in the soft evening air. Along the river a thousand villages are asleep. In his marble palace, flanked by porphyry columns wound with sculptured serpents and crowned with fierce eagles whose eyes flash with precious stones, Egypt's Pharaoh slumbers. In the temples of Isis and Osiris the fire has sunk on the altars and the priests and their attendants are asleep. In the huts and cottages of the peasants the Sons of toil are deep in sleep, sore Labor's bath. In the dungeon the captive has forgotten the galling of his chains as sleep, balm of hurt minds, knits up his raveled sleeve of care. All Egypt is asleep.

The nine plagues are past. The locusts have been swept into the sea, the bane and blisters are healed, new crops are beginning to appear above the ground, the Nile has returned to its clear state, the people hope, and Pharaoh believes that, indeed, they have been delivered from the bane of Moses. He has even uttered a warning: "Get away from me! Take heed to yourself and see my face no more! For in the day you see my face you shall die!" (Exodus 10:28).

And so Egypt sleeps, totally unaware of the horrendous event that is about to befall them. In the villages of the Israelites everything is different. No one sleeps there. Lights are on in every cottage. Inside the people have their robes girt up and tied around their loins—their staffs in their hands. On the tables the roasted Passover lamb with bitter herbs awaits, and the people sit intently listening.

There has been feverish activity that day. There has been the slaying of the lambs, the roasting thereof, and this strange activity where basins of blood have been used to sprinkle the doorposts and lintels of the houses of all of the people.

Even when the blood of the Passover Lamb was spread on the door frame, it made essentially the sign of the cross (the top, with the blood dripping down, and the two sides).

But now all is at rest. And the people wait, and the people listen as midnight draws near.

At length it comes. First is heard a low and distant wailing cry. Then to that is added another and another and another and another until the great crescendo turns into a tidal wave of sorrow and sadness—a wailing cry of anguish. The synonymy of

171

sorrow sweeps over the land of Egypt as the first-born of every household dies—from the Pharaoh in his palace to the peasant in his cottage, to the priest in his temple, to the prisoner in the dungeon, to the cattle in the field. There is naught but death, death, death. Everywhere is death, for the hand of God has struck, and the night and hour of retribution has come.

Years before, an angry Pharaoh had said that the male children of the Israelites were to be taken and cast into the Nile. They were to be killed. So there went forth from every cottage of Israel a similar wailing cry as infants were wrenched from the arms of their mothers by the servants of Pharaoh and cast into the hungry Nile, which one day would turn to blood—an emblem of that ghastly event.

But while all of those horrors were taking place, there stands God behind the shadows keeping watch over His own. Now the cup of Egypt's iniquity is filled to the brim, and the hour has come, and the retribution falls. In this case, as is often the case, it came in kind: Firstborn for firstborn.

From this awful night of doom, there is a great lesson for us, because here God has painted a great mural for us of the salvation of God. In the Bible, Egypt is a picture of this world—this world of sin, this world of bondage, this world of woe, this world of death. Pharaoh is a picture of Satan, who holds a whole world in bondage because of sin. Moses was a great type of Christ, who was to lead his people out of the land of bondage into a greater promised land. In the book of Revelation, we see these plagues repeated on a world-wide scale before Christ leads His people into the promised land.

THE INNOCENT SUBSTITUTE: A LAMB

How was that to be done? The instructions were clear. The command was plain. "Take a lamb." It was to be done by the simple innocence of a lamb—the lamb, which was the type of Christ, the

The Firstborn Slain

innocent substitute. "For the wages of sin is death" (Romans 6:23). The penalty must be paid, but love provided a substitute.

It must be, we were told, a lamb without spot or blemish. The lamb must be perfect. Jesus Christ, the great antitype, was that perfect Lamb, that Lamb without spot or blemish. Peter asseverated, "[Y]ou were not redeemed with corruptible things, like silver or gold

173

… but with the precious blood of Christ, as of a lamb without blemish and without spot" (1 Peter 1:18a, 19).

The Lamb was to be taken on the tenth day of the month and kept until the fourteenth day, when it was to be killed. Why? That it might be observed to be without blemish and without spot. So our Lord Jesus Christ, the great Lamb of God, was on public display for three and a half years, and the people had every opportunity to see if there was blemish or spot. But He was found to be the One and only person who ever walked this earth who had none of the above. He was the Crystal Christ, the altogether Perfect One, the Pure and Undefiled.

And so it was the conclusion of all who knew Him:

- Even the demons said, "I know who You are—the Holy One of God!" (Mark 1:24; Luke 4:34).
- The people said, "He has done all things well" (Mark 7:37).
- Pilate, who condemned Him, said, "I find no fault in Him" (John 19:4).
- The centurion who nailed Him to the Cross said, "Certainly this was a righteous Man!" (Luke 23:47).
- The thief who died before Him said, "This Man has done nothing wrong" (Luke 23:41).
- Even God testified, "This is My beloved Son, in whom I am well pleased" (Matthew 3:17).

He was the perfect, spotless Lamb of God. But that Lamb must die. No living lamb could deliver the people of Israel from Egypt. The lamb must die, for the wages of sin is death, and the wages must be paid. People talk about the life of Christ and, indeed, it is a wonder. His love, His kindness, His gentleness, His grace, His moral purity are the wonder of the world. Yet a living Christ could have saved no one. He had to die.

And so we testify every Sunday when we confess the Apostles' Creed. What does it say about the life of Jesus? It says nothing at all: "He was conceived by the Holy Ghost, born of the Virgin Mary, suffered under Pontius Pilate, was crucified, dead, and buried." The creed makes a gigantic leap from the day of His birth to the day of His death, because He was the Lamb born to die—slain before the foundation of the world.

Not only must the lamb be killed, but the lamb must be roasted with fire. The fire in the Scripture, of course, is a picture of the wrath of God. The Bible makes clear that the wrath of God will fall upon the sins of man, that God is angry with the wicked every day, that God is of purer eyes than to look upon iniquity, and that every sin ever committed will meet with that wrath of God which will consume it and purge the universe of sin. The only question is whether that wrath will meet with your sins while they are on you, in Hell, or when they are on Christ at Calvary. The choice is yours.

The Scripture makes it plain that life is in the blood, and without the shedding of blood, there is no forgiveness of sins. Take a lamb, said God. But there must be application, as well, and so we are told to take the blood—the blood of the lamb.

CONCLUSION

It is interesting to note that no blood was to be placed upon the threshold, just the sides and the top of the door frames. And, said God, "When I see the blood, I will pass over your houses." In one sense, every day is Passover night. The angel of death will visit more homes this night, by far, than were visited in Egypt that night long ago. The angel stands poised to enter homes this very night. Will he see the blood upon the door? Each of us should make sure we are covered by the blood of Jesus, the true Passover Lamb.

CHAPTER 25

The Risen One

⚬⚬⚬

PROPHECY:

*For You will not leave my soul in Sheol, nor will You allow Your Holy
One to see corruption*.*
Psalm 16:10

FULFILLMENT:

*"For David says concerning Him: 'I foresaw the Lord always before
my face, for He is at my right hand, that I may not be shaken. Therefore my heart rejoiced, and my tongue was glad; moreover my flesh
also will rest in hope. For You will not leave my soul in Hades, nor will
You allow Your Holy One to see corruption.* You have made known
to me the ways of life; You will make me full of joy in Your presence.'
Men and brethren, let me speak freely to you of the patriarch David,
that he is both dead and buried, and his tomb is with us to this day.
Therefore, being a prophet, and knowing that God had sworn with an
oath to him that of the fruit of his body, according to the flesh, He
would raise up the Christ to sit on his throne, he, foreseeing this, spoke
concerning the resurrection of the Christ, that His soul was not left in
Hades, nor did His flesh see corruption. This Jesus God has raised up,
of which we are all witnesses."*
Acts 2:25–32

* Note: "Corruption" in this context means decay.

The resurrection of Christ is the best established fact of antiquity. I have never met a person who has read so much as one book on the evidences for the resurrection of Christ who did not believe that it happened. I have met many people who did not believe in the resurrection, but they have never examined the evidence. A nineteenyear-old young man once said to me, "Well, it's just your opinion. There's no evidence to support it." However, this is not the case. The resurrection is an article of faith which is strongly supported by historical fact.

Dr. Simon Greenleaf (1783-1853) was highly qualified to examine such evidence. He was the Royal Professor of Law at Harvard University and was declared by the Chief Justice of the Supreme Court of the United States to be the greatest authority on legal evidence who had ever lived. Dr. Greenleaf was considered by many to be the highest authority on evidence that could be quoted in any Englishspeaking courtroom in the world. After writing voluminously on the laws of legal evidence, he decided to turn the searchlight of his knowledge and his ability to discern truth from falsehood to the resurrection of Christ.

He minutely examined each thread of evidence concerning the resurrection and concluded that if any unbiased courtroom in the world were presented with the evidence, they would adjudge the resurrection of Christ to be an absolute historical fact. This was the opinion of the greatest authority on evidence that the world has ever known—Dr. Simon Greenleaf of Harvard.

What was the evidence Dr. Greenleaf studied? Although there are many details, the evidence can be organized into two main categories.

The first category consists of the complete lack of any other reasonable explanation for the disappearance of Christ's body from the tomb. Christ was killed and placed in a tomb carved from solid rock that was guarded by soldiers and had the seal of Rome upon it. Anyone breaking that seal would be guilty of a crime punishable by death.

Skeptics have developed many explanations concerning how

The Resurrection

Christ's body disappeared from the sealed tomb. One such idea is that Jesus swooned on the Cross, revived while in the grave, and pushed aside the stone—which had taken several men to roll into place. Another theory is that the fearfilled disciples stole the body. Each of these hypotheses is filled with difficulties and inconsistencies. Neither is a possible explanation in light of all the historical facts. Only a resurrection fully explains the disappearance of the body of Christ from a guarded tomb and His subsequent appearance to over 500 people after His death (1 Corinthians 15).

The second category of evidence for the resurrection is the changed lives of the apostles. In forty days, these men who were afraid to suffer with their leader were transformed into bold and fearless witnesses. Most of the apostles were eventually condemned to a martyr's death. To believe that the apostles would suffer persecution and death for what they knew to be a lie is beyond credible belief. Moreover, it is hard to believe that men of such integrity and religious fervor would purposely preach a lie.

CONCLUSION

A careful examination of the historical and biblical evidence proves that Jesus Christ has risen from the grave and is alive today. Jesus is not a dead martyr but a living Savior and Lord. Our Christian faith is based on facts and is reasonable. To reject Christ is to be at war with reality. It is the Christian and not the skeptic who can point to the facts of history to support his view of Jesus Christ.

In the early Church, one Christian would often greet another follower of Jesus with this declaration: "He is risen!"

The second person would respond in turn, "He is risen, indeed!" Amen.

CHAPTER 26

A Priest in the Order of Melchizedek

❦

PROPHECY:

The Lord has sworn and will not relent, "You are a priest forever according to the order of Melchizedek."

Psalm 110:4

FULFILLMENT:

So also Christ did not glorify Himself to become High Priest, but it was He who said to Him: "You are My Son, today I have begotten You." As He also says in another place: "You are a priest forever according to the order of Melchizedek."

Hebrews 5:5–6

Who is Melchizedek? What relationship does he have with Jesus Christ? To answer these questions, it is necessary for us to review some Old Testament history in light of the new revelation, which has come with the victorious work of Jesus Christ.

Melchizedek first appears after God granted Abraham and his "army" of 300 servants a great victory over five kings who had vastly superior military forces. Melchizedek, "a priest of the Most High God" and "King of Salem," came out to meet Abraham and was given a tenth of the spoil of the battle. He then blessed Abraham and shared a meal of bread and wine with him. Bread and wine? Here is a foreshadowing of the Lord's Table.

Melchizedek is a man of mystery in the Old Testament. He appears out of nowhere, he has no genealogy, and his death is not recorded. He was honored by the Father of the covenant people, Abraham, and blessed him. Psalm 110 indicates that Melchizedek is a foreshadowing of the King/Priest who would fulfill the Messianic promises given to David.

In Israel, the offices of King and Priest were always kept separate. King Saul lost his throne because he dared to assume the role of the priest, Samuel, and offer sacrifices to God. God separated the two offices to limit the sin of fallen man, just as our Constitution has established three branches of government to limit political corruption. Only the Messiah, who would follow the order of Melchizedek, would be entrusted and honored with both of these offices.

Melchizedek's name means "King of righteousness," and he was also called the "King of Peace" (Hebrews 7:2). Both of these names are Messianic titles and refer to Jesus' role as God's anointed.

The prophecy of a King/Priest is continually fulfilled by Jesus Christ, for He has offered Himself as the final and perfect atonement for the sins of His people. He is in constant prayer before the throne of God on our behalf, bringing to us God's blessing and grace. He has sent the Spirit to teach us His will and has granted us forgiveness and communion with God.

CONCLUSION

This truth should greatly affect our prayer life and allow us to come "boldly" before God and ask for His grace and strength when we are in the midst of trials (Hebrews 4:16). Christ is our only mediator. We must come to God the Father through Him alone (1 Timothy 2:5–6). With Jesus at the right hand of God as the King/Priest of the new covenant, the believer need not fear. God's throne is a haven of mercy.

CHAPTER 27

The Kingdom Established

ⓈⓍⓈ

PROPHECY:
You have ascended on high, You have led captivity captive; You have received gifts among men, even from the rebellious, that the Lord God might dwell there.
Psalm 68:18

FULFILLMENT:
"When He ascended on high, He led captivity captive, and gave gifts to men."
Ephesians 4:8

Would we have reacted any differently? One moment Jesus was speaking to them about the Kingdom of God and the Holy Spirit; the next He was moving toward the heavens where a cloud enveloped Him and blocked Him from their sight. Wouldn't we also stand there gazing toward the heavens?

Yet, even as the apostles had difficulty at first understanding the ascension of Christ into Heaven, many Christians today still do not understand its great importance to their daily lives. The ascension of Christ is a crucial act in God's redemption of His creation and the establishment of His Kingdom.

The Ascension

With the ascension of Christ, God established the Messianic Kingdom. This Kingdom has existed ever since Jesus was received back into Heaven and granted the Davidic throne (Revelation 3:7; 5:5–9). All the rulers of the earth are now accountable to Christ (Revelation 1:5).

As the heavenly King, Jesus has commissioned believers as ambassadors to go out and teach, baptize, and disciple all nations (Matthew 28:19–20). Christ promises His people that all authority and power are now in His hands and that His presence will be with them wherever they go. He has guaranteed that His message will never be proclaimed in vain.

As the Gospel is preached and believed, Satan's power in the world diminishes, and his activities are restricted. Through the "foolishness" of the preaching of the Gospel, God has chosen to create a universal nation of believers whose "citizens" have accepted Christ as their Lord and Savior. This nation of believers shall bring glory to God and have dominion over all the earth. All of this rests upon Christ's ascension and claim to the Messianic throne.

It is vital that we recognize the victory that Christ won on the Cross (Colossians 2). When we understand the impact of this great spiritual victory, we will be able to perceive the government of God on this earth and the advance of God's Kingdom—even in the most difficult of times.

The victory of Christ and His ascension leads us to the reality that, although persecuted and rejected by the world, the Christian Church will continue to grow and prosper until God's Kingdom is fully manifested on earth. At the return of Christ, the Church shall be seen in all of its glory and shall be freed from the punishment, power, and presence of sin for all eternity. The people of God shall be purified and shall enjoy perfect fellowship with Christ for all eternity.

CONCLUSION

Therefore, we must not despair. The promise of the Messiah's ascension and Jesus' fulfillment of the prophecy assures us that our labor is "not in vain in the Lord" (1 Corinthians 15:58). We must press on in every front—whether personal, social, political, ecclesiastical, intellectual, domestic, or educational—to see Christ, His Gospel, and His law honored and obeyed. God's Kingdom will rule on earth, even as it does in Heaven. As we say in the Lord's prayer: "For the kingdom, the power, and the glory are yours. Now and forever. Amen."

The Gospel According to Isaiah

INTRODUCTION

Of all of the writers of the Old Testament, the Hebrew prophet Isaiah clearly says more about the coming Messiah than any other. We find in the book of Isaiah more than 25 prophecies concerning Christ written over 700 years before He was born. That is why it is sometimes called the Gospel of Isaiah. The following chapters contain several of these Messianic prophecies.

The Gospels were written in the first century. Yet, in a sense, one could argue that the first Gospel was written in the 8th century B.C. It is the Gospel of Isaiah where the Good News of Jesus Christ was first spelled out in many details. These details include:

- His eternal nature,
- His divinity,
- His family lineage,
- His Virgin Birth,
- That He would preach Good News to the poor and downtrodden,
- His ministry of miracles (giving sight to the blind, hearing to the deaf, etc.),
- His scourging and suffering and death for our sins,
- His resurrection from the dead,
- That He would be a light for the Gentiles, and
- That His kingdom would spread, gaining adherents all over the world.

As we will see in the following chapters, virtually everything we need to know about Jesus, we can learn from Isaiah.

The Prophet Isaiah

CHAPTER 28

The Virgin Birth

❦

PROPHECY:
*"Therefore the Lord Himself will give you a sign: Behold, the virgin
shall conceive and bear a Son, and shall call His name Immanuel."*
Isaiah 7:14

FULFILLMENT:
*"Behold, the virgin shall be with child, and bear a Son, and they shall
call His name Immanuel," which is translated, "God with us."*
Matthew 1:23

A young American minister, freshly minted from a theological
seminary, went out to take his first pastorate. It was a little church
out in the country in an area mostly populated by Scandinavian folk,
and the young man was filled with great zeal and hope.

He noticed that in the area there lived an elderly gentleman who
apparently did not attend church at all. One day the young pastor
invited him to attend, and he refused. The next week he invited the
man again, and finally he agreed. He picked him up and drove the
man to church. His sermon happened to be on the same topic of this
chapter, which is the Virgin Birth of Christ. As he was driving him
back home, the minister made a foolish mistake only made by very

young preachers. He said, "Well, how did you like the sermon?"

The elderly man was silent for a while, but he finally said, "Well now, young man, if there was a young girl that got herself pregnant today, and then you were told that it was a virgin birth, would you believe that?"

The young pastor was quiet for a moment, and then he said, "Well, if that Child grew up to live a sinless life, the only life that men have never been able to find fault with; if He worked numerous extraordinary miracles; if He raised the dead; walked on water; and if He Himself, having been crucified, rose again from the dead and then ascended into Heaven, yes, I would believe that He was Virgin born."

The Virgin Birth is truly remarkable when we think about it. Science tells us that every effect requires an adequate cause. One thing the Hebrew people knew far better than any other people in the world was that we were part of a fallen race—that man had sinned against God and was born with a corrupt nature. As soon as man was old enough to exercise it, he would continue that sin. They were quite familiar with the words along these lines:

- "There is none who does good, no, not one" (Psalm 14:3).
- "All we like sheep have gone astray; we have turned, every one, to his own way" (Isaiah 53:6).
- "The heart is deceitful above all things, and desperately wicked; who can know it?" (Jeremiah 17:9) . . . and many other such texts.

They knew that all men were sinful. Then suddenly there appears One who was not. No one has ever been able to find sin in Him. He boldly asked, "Which of you convicts Me of sin?" (John 8:46).

Jesus was tempted in all ways, such as we are, yet He remained without sin. He could say, "… I do always those things that please him [my Father]" (John 8:29). Can any of us say that? He was the peerless, stainless, Crystal Christ, the only unblemished person who ever lived. What is the sufficient cause for such an astonishing effect? The answer, of course, is that He was virgin born, and the stain of Adam's sin, which has infected the human race, did not come to Him.

SATAN'S ATTACKS

It seems as if the devil does not like that idea very well. He did not like it from the very beginning. As we saw earlier, the first promise of a virgin-born person coming into this world was given to Satan when God said that the seed of the woman, whom Satan had just deceived into sin, would destroy his head. So Satan had long been on the lookout for such a One, and his followers have indeed done their best to help.

Some of you might remember the name of a famous liberal minister of the earlier part of the twentieth century, Harry Emerson Fosdick, who preached at the prestigious, liberal Riverside Church in New York City. He was preaching a sermon on the Virgin Birth, and these are the words with which he began his sermon: "I want to assure you that I do not believe in the Virgin Birth, and I hope that none of you do either."

I would imagine that he had their attention. By the way, Fosdick led the charge of liberalism in America in the twentieth century. Many other ministers followed in his train of thought. In fact, I was told that a minister in a local church preached a similar sermon years ago in his church. It was not too long after that that he was put out to pasture as an alcoholic.

One theologian said that he had never known any Christian who denied the Virgin Birth who was not off on many other aspects of the life, person, and work of Jesus Christ. Yes, it is an important matter. It goes all the way back to the very beginning, when the first promise of God, the *protevangelium*, the first evangel, the first Gospel, was given that the seed of the woman would bruise the head of the seed of the serpent.

The Annunciation to Mary

PROPHECIES

No one can say that the text of Isaiah 7:14 was ever changed. In fact, a copy of the scroll of Isaiah was found complete in the Dead Sea Scrolls, which was copied before Christ was born. I have seen the copy and read parts of it in Jerusalem. Here we have such things as, "Behold, the virgin shall conceive . . ." (Isaiah 7:14), and "For unto us a Child is born, unto us a Son is given" (Isaiah 9:6). Notice: A *Child* was born; a *Son* was given.

The Bible teaches the Virgin Birth very clearly. The New Testament is quite explicit. In the book of Matthew, we have the genealogies. Abraham begot, begot, begot. David begot, begot. Finally, down to a second Jacob, and Jacob begot Joseph, who begot Jesus. *No.* Rather, it says, "And Jacob begot Joseph the husband of Mary, of whom (feminine pronoun in Greek) was born Jesus, who is called Christ" (Matthew 1:16).

Is this not the son of Joseph, they said, as it was supposed? Scripture makes it very clear He was not, but He was thought to be. Mary, herself, made it abundantly clear, when the angel Gabriel announced that she was going to conceive and have a child. She said, "How can this be, since I do not know a man?" (Luke 1:34).

Yet, some liberal theologians still try to get rid of the Virgin Birth, and they often do it by saying that it is really not important— that it does not make any difference. The word "liberal" comes from the Latin term that means "to cut loose," as to liberate from slavery. In politics, it is the cutting loose from the historic text of the Constitution. In theology, it means to cut loose from the moorings of the Scriptures and all of the ancient Creeds of the Church and go one's own way.

IS IT IMPORTANT?

So the liberals will say that the Virgin Birth really does not matter. It is not important. I sat down one time and thought about that. Is the Virgin Birth of Christ really important, or does it really not make much difference? Here are some of the differences it makes that came to my mind in probably only 15 minutes:

1. If Jesus was not born of a virgin, the New Testament narratives are proved untrue and unreliable.
2. Mary is stained with the sin of unchastity.
3. Jesus was mistaken about His own paternity. He just thought He was the Son of God.

4. Christ was not born of the seed of the woman and is not the fulfillment of the ancient *protevangelium* (Genesis 3:15).
5. Jesus was, then, an illegitimate child.
6. He is consequently not the God-man or the Son of God.
7. He was, then, a sinner just like the rest of us.
8. As a sinner, He could not have been the divine Redeemer.
9. Therefore, we have no Savior at all.
10. We are yet in our sins and without forgiveness and are under the condemnation of God Almighty.
11. We have no hope after death.
12. There is no mediator between God and man.
13. There is no Trinity because there is no second person of the Trinity.
14. Christ should have prayed, "Father, forgive us," not "them."
15. Lastly, if this miracle is denied, why not deny them all? C. S. Lewis called the incarnation "the grand miracle" because, he argues, this miracle makes other miracles possible.

ARGUMENT FROM SILENCE

What excuse do theologians give for denying the Virgin Birth? I will tell you a little story. It happened in a Presbytery meeting of the Presbyterian Church U.S.A. One time, a young man was being examined for ordination and during that examination, he admitted that he did not believe in the Virgin Birth.

That woke up the audience, and other ministers began to question him more closely about the matter until one older minister stood up and said, "Now, gentlemen, do not be too harsh on this young man. After all, it's not really important. The fact of the matter is, I do not believe in the Virgin Birth myself."

Everyone really sat up after that admission. One other minister asked, "For goodness sake, why not?"

He said, "Very simply, it's only mentioned in Matthew and Luke. It's not found in Mark or John at all, and furthermore, in none of the epistles of Paul is the Virgin Birth ever alluded to. Therefore, I don't believe in any Virgin Birth at all."

Then Dr. Harry Rimmer (now deceased) stood up. He had a doctorate in theology and another doctorate in science. He asked, "May I ask you then, sir, what is it that you preach?"

He answered, "I preach the Sermon on the Mount. There's enough religion in that for me."

Dr. Rimmer said, "There's not enough for me." That really shocked everyone, because he was a paragon of orthodoxy.

The older minister queried, "Why not?"

He responded, "Because I don't believe that Jesus ever preached any Sermon on the Mount." (This was getting to be an exciting Presbytery meeting.)

The older liberal said, "For heaven's sakes, why would you say a thing like that?"

Dr. Rimmer answered, "It's very simple. The Sermon on the Mount is only mentioned in Matthew and Luke [the same two books that mention the Virgin Birth]. It's not mentioned at all in the Gospel of Mark or in the Gospel of John, and furthermore, the apostle Paul, in all of his letters never once alludes to it at all. Therefore, I don't believe there ever was anything such as the Sermon on the Mount."

At that point, the old liberal sat down. It was the death knell for his argument, which is known as "the argument from silence." It is often used, and it is the weakest of all possible arguments. You can prove almost anything by the argument from silence. What would you like for me to prove from the argument from silence?

May I say to you, for example, in the Gospel of Mark, not only does Mark never mention the Virgin Birth, Mark never mentions the birth of Christ at all. Therefore, Mark did not believe that Jesus had ever been born—period. That is the argument from silence.

Take the miracles of Christ. What does Paul have to say about the miracles of Christ? Nothing. Not in any one of his epistles. Ergo, Jesus never worked any miracles. What about the parables? Again, what did Paul say about them? Nothing. Therefore, Jesus never told any parables. Goodbye Good Samaritan, goodbye Prodigal Son, goodbye to all the parables and all the miracles, to all of the Sermon on the Mount. With the argument from silence, you can get rid of almost anything—and that is why it is really no argument at all.

WHAT ABOUT MIRACLES?

Of course, there are those who would want to get rid of miracles altogether and say that they do not believe in any miracles whatsoever. What should we say to them? If you ask them why not, and if they are knowledgeable, they will probably tell you, "Well, David Hume demolished miracles."

Hume was a Scottish philosopher a couple of centuries ago. He wrote a very devastating attack on miracles—at least it has been taken as such by many people since then, and many believe that he got rid of miracles.

I do not know if you have ever studied Hume's writings on miracles, but they are interesting. He said that the basic thrust of his argument was that in the entire fixed and solid history of the human race, there has never been known anyone to have done a miracle. Therefore, if someone comes along and says that he has performed a miracle or that he has seen someone perform a miracle, you have a choice—either the entire uniform history of mankind is wrong or this person is either mistaken or lying. What are the probabilities, he asks. He concludes that the probabilities are overwhelmingly in favor of the entire history of the human race and against this one man. Therefore, that miracle never happened.

I wonder how many of you see the flaws in that argument? First of all, let me point out to you that there are thousands of people in history who have proclaimed that they have seen miracles. Throughout the Old Testament and the New Testament, thousands of people witnessed all kinds of miracles.

What do you do? First of all, you get rid of all of them, and then you say you have a unanimous "unified history" of the human race, having gotten rid of everyone who disagrees with your point of view. If a person comes and says, "I have seen a miracle," you remove that person from the equation. Therefore, you can say, "No one has ever seen a miracle, except those that have seen a miracle."

Furthermore, Hume bases his argument upon probabilities. If you have hundreds of millions of people who have uniformly never seen a miracle, and you have this one person claiming to have seen a miracle, what are the probabilities as to which would be right? Are they not overwhelmingly in favor of the great mass of people?

But let me tell you something here, if you do not already know it: *probabilities* have nothing whatsoever to do with miracles. When we say we believe in a miracle—that Christ rose from the dead, for example, or whatever it is—do we mean that out of 275,643,412 people, one of them is going to rise from the dead? Or do you change the figure to anything you would like? Of course not.

Probabilities have nothing to do with miracles. Miracles have to do with the divine will of the omnipotent sovereign God, who will raise anyone He wants from the dead at any time He wishes and cannot be examined probabilistically at all. It is a totally fallacious argument, yet there are still some who refer to Hume as the great destroyer of miracles. That will not work. A miracle is a miracle be-cause it is extra-ordinary. It does not happen usually, and it cannot be duplicated. It is an intervention of the divine into the temporal.

CONCLUSION

It is interesting, I think, that there is no doubt that there was one person on this earth who absolutely, positively, one hundred percent knew whether or not Jesus was born of a virgin, and that was Mary. That was the same Mary who raised this little Boy to man-hood, the same Mary who loved Him with a love like any other mother would have for her Son, the same Mary that came to Cal-vary and looked up into the face of her dear, dear beloved Son, who was agonizing on those spikes on the Cross.

She, all by herself, could have stopped that. Why was He being crucified? Because He claimed to be the Son of God. She could have said, "Stop, and I'll tell you who His Father was. It was … whatever name you want." Is there any mother who, to save her own reputation, would watch her Son die horribly, agonizingly, excruciatingly, and say nothing? There is none, and yet she said nothing, because she absolutely knew that He was born of a virgin, and that He was, as Gabriel said, the Son of God.

CHAPTER 29

The Rise and Fall of Many

❧

PROPHECY:
"And many among them shall stumble; they shall fall and be broken,
be snared and taken."
Isaiah 8:15

FULFILLMENT:
Then Simeon blessed them, and said to Mary His mother, "Behold,
this Child is destined for the fall and rising of many in Israel, and for
a sign which will be spoken against."
Luke 2:34

This prophecy in Isaiah can be seen clearly in the Gospels. Wherever Jesus went, there were those who loved Him and those who opposed Him. Those who rejected Him were rejecting God Himself. Thus, He was the cause of people stumbling.

Why did they reject Him? Because of their own sin. That was true then; that is true today. Jesus summed it up so well: Light has come into the world but men prefer darkness because their deeds are evil (John 3:20).

Jesus said He did not come to bring peace, but a sword. That is, wherever His message goes, some believe and some do not, and so they become divided. He brings salvation to those who accept Him. Those who reject Him are condemned already, because they will be punished for their own sins, instead of letting Him take on the punishment for their sins.

Matthew Henry notes about Isaiah 8:15: "What was a savour of life unto life to others would be a savour of death unto death to them."[45]

Here is the perspective from *The Navarre Bible Commentary*:

> Jesus came to bring salvation to all men, yet he will be a sign of contradiction because some people will obstinately reject him—and for this reason he will be their ruin. But for those who accept him with faith, Jesus will be their salvation, freeing them from sin in this life and raising them up to eternal life.[46]

Jesus brings out the truth that is in us. I have seen some seemingly gracious and reasonable people change for the worse when the name of Jesus is mentioned in front of them. They change when rubbed with the Touchstone of Christ in the life of some devoted believer. The tiger comes out and the claws are extended; they show their natural animosity to God.

Christ is the Touchstone of human character. What we really are in the depths of our souls is revealed by our encounter with Him. I remember a lovely lady who often waited upon my wife and I when we visited a certain store. She was a pure delight. She was lovely of face and figure and had a marvelous personality. She was exceedingly gracious and yet dignified and friendly and warm. One day my wife, while visiting the store, entered into a conversation with the lady and my wife brought up the subject of Christ and her relationship to Him.

My wife, in relating the incident to me, said, "The strangest thing happened. This woman seemed to be transfigured before my eyes, and her countenance was changed. She became glaringly opposed to all that I was saying." Her true nature was revealed. Christ is the touchstone of the real character of our soul.

CONCLUSION

Isaiah foretold that Jesus would not only be the cause of many to rise. But he also saw that Jesus would cause others to fall. Those who reject Him are in eternal peril.

We can see clearly that the Pharisees and Sadducees could not accept the fact that God in the flesh was right before their eyes. They rejected Him, to their own demise. Meanwhile, tax collectors, women of ill repute, and other sinners were flocking to Jesus and putting their faith in Him. All of this was foretold by Isaiah long before it came to pass.

CHAPTER 30

A Light for the Gentiles

❦

PROPHECY:

Nevertheless, there will be no more gloom, for those who were in distress. In the past He humbled the land of Zebulun and the land of Naphtali, but in the future He will honor Galilee of the Gentiles, by the way of the sea, along the Jordan—The people walking in darkness have seen a great light; on those living in the land of the shadow of death a light has dawned.
Isaiah 9:1-2 NIV

FULFILLMENT:

And leaving Nazareth, He came and dwelt in Capernaum, which is by the sea, in the regions of Zebulun and Naphtali, that it might be fulfilled which was spoken by Isaiah the prophet, saying: "The land of Zebulun and the land of Naphtali, by the way of the sea, beyond the Jordan, Galilee of the Gentiles: The people who sat in darkness have seen a great light, and upon those who sat in the region and shadow of death light has dawned."
Matthew 4:13–16

The Assyrian hordes thundered across the region of Zebulun and Naphtali, the northern area of Israel. Destruction and defeat surrounded the Israelites. Yet, the prophet Isaiah indicates in this passage that though they were oppressed, their land would one day become the homeland of the Messiah.

This prophecy is interesting for a number of reasons. First of all, it again shows God's control over the details of history. Hundreds of years before Jesus came to earth, God had already pointed out the region of Israel in which the Messiah would conduct the majority of His ministry. God is able to control the events of history and mold them to accomplish His plan. This should fortify our trust in God.

Second, this passage hints at the deliverance that Christ would provide, not just for the believing remnant of Israel, but for the people of God found in all nations (Acts 15:16–17). Isaiah proclaimed that the great revelation of the incarnate Christ was centered in an area known as "Galilee of the Gentiles." Here is just the beginning of a suggestion that God's salvation would reach all nations and peoples. The light of Christ would cover the earth and reach every kindred, tongue, people, and nation. So great is God's grace and love that He designed to share it with every segment of mankind.

Finally, this passage is fascinating because Isaiah is expecting to comfort people who are facing immediate disaster with a future promise of deliverance. He wants them to know that they do not need to despair. The final act of the play does not leave God's people defeated and destroyed. No. God's great deliverer will come and bring light to a land of darkness. God will redeem His people.

This indicates to us that we, too, must look at our present problems and trials in the light of the final victory of Christ over all of His enemies. Though we may be oppressed and see no human means of deliverance, our trust must remain in Jesus Christ (James 1:1–12). He is aware of our current problems and will bring justice to His people upon His return (James 5:1–7).

CONCLUSION

Jesus Christ is "the true Light which gives light to every man coming into the world" (John 1:9). He can turn our lives from despair to hope, from doubt to faith, from frustration to love. When we call upon Him in the hour of need, He will not fail to answer us. He will be our light.

CHAPTER 31

For Unto Us A Child Is Born

❧

PROPHECY:

For unto us a Child is born, unto us a Son is given; and the govern-
ment will be upon His shoulder. And His name will be called Wonder-
ful, Counselor, Mighty God, Everlasting Father, Prince of Peace. Of the
increase of His government and peace there will be no end, upon the
throne of David and over His kingdom, to order it and establish it
with judgment and justice from that time forward, even forever. The
zeal of the Lord of hosts will perform this.
Isaiah 9:6–7

FULFILLMENT:

"He will be great, and will be called the Son of the Highest; and the
Lord God will give Him the throne of His father David. And He will
reign over the house of Jacob forever, and of His kingdom there will be
no end."
Luke 1:32–33

Isaiah's prophecy of the coming Child who would sit upon David's throne is a vivid declaration of the person of Christ and the nature of His Kingdom. Here we have summarized for us the nature of Jesus Christ and the marvelous truth of the incarnation.

Some unbelievers have charged Christianity with changing the Old Testament vision of the Messiah. They claim that the Old Testament speaks only of a national deliverer who would be an extraordinary man—and yet just a man, and not God. However, a careful study of the titles that Isaiah uses in this prophecy declares that the coming Messiah would be God in the flesh.

The first titles attributed to Christ are "Wonderful" and "Counselor." In Isaiah 28:29, it is revealed that it is Yahweh, the Creator God, who is "wonderful in counsel." It is clear that the prophet Isaiah thought of these terms as divine attributes that the Messiah would possess.

Isaiah then stated clearly that the coming Christ (or Messiah) would be, in fact, "The Mighty God." This same term is used again in Isaiah 10:21, referring to God. This is an amazing Old Testament prophecy, which undeniably declares that the coming Messiah is not merely a great man, but God in the flesh.

It was the Son of God who came and who was incarnated in human flesh in the womb of Mary. "... His name will be called Wonderful, Counselor, Mighty God, Everlasting Father, Prince of Peace" (Isaiah 9:6). The Mighty God is going to be born into human life. It is the most spectacular, astonishing thing that the world has ever known. We are the visited planet. The Creator of the galaxies has visited this world, and He came, astonishing to say, to die for the creatures' sin.

The vision of the coming Messiah continues in its astounding clarity, as Isaiah paradoxically proclaimed this child "The Everlasting Father." This term also refers to the Messiah as God, and it indicates that He would be a kind and benevolent ruler of His people, demonstrating both paternal wisdom and love (Isaiah 9:6; Malachi 2:10).

The final name given the promised Messiah by Isaiah is "Prince of Peace." This Prince of Peace will bring God's perfect rule to the earth. He will establish a Kingdom where true justice and righteousness dwell. This will be accomplished by the zeal of the Lord of hosts.

CONCLUSION

The Old Testament foretold of a Messiah who would not only be a deliverer of His people, but a full manifestation of almighty God. This becomes clear as we see the titles ascribed to Christ. Christians, therefore, should be confident in their witness of the incarnation, knowing that they are in full agreement with the Old Testament revelation.

CHAPTER 32

The Son of David

⚜

PROPHECY:

*Of the increase of His government and peace there will be no end,
upon the throne of David and over His kingdom, to order it and establish it with judgment and justice from that time forward, even forever. The zeal of the Lord of hosts will perform this."*
Isaiah 9:7

*There shall come forth a Rod from the stem of Jesse, and a Branch
shall grow out of his roots. The Spirit of the Lord shall rest upon Him,
the Spirit of wisdom and understanding, the Spirit of counsel and
might, the Spirit of knowledge and of the fear of the Lord. His delight
is in the fear of the Lord, and He shall not judge by the sight of His
eyes, nor decide by the hearing of His ears; but with righteousness He
shall judge the poor, and decide with equity for the meek of the earth;
He shall strike the earth with the rod of His mouth, and with the
breath of His lips He shall slay the wicked. Righteousness shall be the
belt of His loins, and faithfulness the belt of His waist. The wolf also
shall dwell with the lamb, the leopard shall lie down with the young
goat, the calf and the young lion and the fatling together; and a little
child shall lead them. The cow and the bear shall graze; their young
ones shall lie down together; and the lion shall eat straw like the ox.
The nursing child shall play by the cobra's hole, and the weaned child*

shall put his hand in the viper's den. They shall not hurt nor destroy in all My holy mountain, for the earth shall be full of the knowledge of the Lord as the waters cover the sea. And in that day there shall be a Root of Jesse, who shall stand as a banner to the people; for the Gentiles shall seek Him, and His resting place shall be glorious. It shall come to pass in that day that the Lord shall set His hand again the second time to recover the remnant of His people who are left, from Assyria and Egypt, from Pathros and Cush, from Elam and Shinar, from Hamath and the islands of the sea. He will set up a banner for the nations, and will assemble the outcasts of Israel, and gather together the dispersed of Judah from the four corners of the earth.
Isaiah 11:1-12

FULFILLMENT:
Jesus ... the Son of Jesse....
Luke 3:23, 32

"... the Christ is the Son of David...."
Mark 12:35

As foretold by the Hebrew prophets, Jesus Christ is the Son of David. We want to explore the importance of His genealogies. It seems singularly strange to Western ears to have a book begin with a genealogy, as does the Gospel of Matthew. That is just not the way that we are accustomed to doing things. Yet, before we dismiss it as merely an Oriental peculiarity, we should remember that these genealogies, with which the Bible abounds, are vital to God's plan for bringing the Messiah into the world and for identifying Him as such.

It was not primarily to the astounding miracles wrought by Christ that the apostles appealed for proof of His Messiahship, though these stunned their minds and wrung from their lips the cry, "What manner of man is this?" *Nor* yet to the stainless and immaculate purity of His life, as extraordinary as this was and as strikingly as it contrasted with the corruption and pollution of all of his contemporaries—not to mention His antecedents. *Nor even* the life-transforming impact of His ministry on those who believed on Him, though the entire panorama of history offered nothing comparable to the metamorphosis of personality that took place in the lives of those that were confronted by the Christ. *But rather* their primary appeal was to the astonishing correlation of the minutest details of His life to the myriads of explicit Old Testament prophecies of the promised Messiah.

This was especially true in regard to those prophecies which were totally and completely beyond the ability of any imposter to arrange—such as who His parents should be (every person should choose his parents carefully), the place and manner of His birth, His tribe, and His remote ancestors. It should be patently obvious to any person that details such as these are totally beyond the capacity of anyone to arrange.

FASCINATING GENEALOGIES

The genealogies for Christ are found in the first chapter of the Gospel of Matthew and in the third chapter of the Gospel of Luke. In the Gospel of Matthew the genealogy begins with Abraham and works its way down to Christ. In Luke's Gospel, Luke begins with Jesus and goes all the way back through David and Abraham, all the way to Adam, who was the son of God.

Writing primarily for the Jews, Matthew traces our Lord's Abrahamic and Davidic descent; Luke, writing primarily for Gentiles, traces Him all the way up to Adam, as indeed the Son of Man and the inheritor of the whole human race.

The main purpose of these genealogies is to show proof of the Messiahship of Christ. That is done in three ways. First of all, there is the evidence that He is of the seed of Abraham. In Genesis we read that it would be through the seed of Abraham that the whole world would be blessed. The Apostle Paul says in Galatians 3 that that seed was Christ—that He was the seed of Abraham which would come into the world and which would bring the blessings of God upon all the world, through the family of Abraham. The genealogy shows that Jesus was the descendant of Abraham. In fact, it begins with the statement: "Abraham begot Isaac."

Second, it shows that He was also of the tribe of Judah. We already saw in chapter 9 how Jesus fulfilled the prophecy of Genesis 49:10, that the scepter would not leave Judah, nor a lawgiver, until Shiloh (another name for Messiah) would come. Not only must Shiloh come through the tribe of Judah, but He must come before the scepter departed from Judah, before their legal authority as a tribe is removed.

Josephus, a noted Jewish general and historian, in his *Antiquities of the Jews*, describes a most amazing event. He tells us that Rabbi Rachmon said, "When the members of the Sanhedrin found themselves deprived of their right over life and death, a general consternation took possession of them; they covered their heads with ashes and their bodies with sackcloth, exclaiming, 'Woe unto us, for the scepter has departed from Judah and the Messiah has not come.'"

This removal of the right of life and death from the tribe of Judah took place when Archelaus was removed as king and a Roman Pro-Consul was put in his place. This event took place when Judea became a Roman province. Jesus of Nazareth was then eleven years old. Unknown to the Sanhedrin, Shiloh had already come. When that scepter was removed, it was no longer possible for any Messiah to come at a later date. Furthermore, the record house where the genealogical records were kept was destroyed by Titus and Vespasian in 70 A.D., as was the temple nearby. Today it is not possible for any Jew to prove himself to be a descendant of the tribe of Judah.

Third, in addition to showing that Jesus came of the seed of Abraham and that He was of the tribe of Judah, it also proves that He was David's son. This was very important because there are many prophecies in the Old Testament that point to the fact that Messiah must be David's son. We already saw the fulfillment of this prophecy in chapter 31: "For unto us a Child is born, unto us a Son is given; and the government will be upon His shoulder. And His name will be called Wonderful, Counselor, Mighty God, Everlasting Father, Prince of Peace. Of the increase of His government and peace there will be no end, upon *the throne of David* and over His kingdom, to order it and establish it with judgment and justice from that time forward, even forever. The zeal of the Lord of hosts will perform this" (Isaiah 9:6–7, emphasis mine).

So it was very clear to all of the Jews that Messiah would come of the line of David. In Matthew 22:41-42, we read: "While the Pharisees were gathered together, Jesus asked them, saying, 'What do you think about the Christ? Whose Son is He?' They said to Him, 'The Son of David.'" As we look through the New Testament, we see such phrases as these applied to Christ: "the Son of David;" "of the seed of David;" "Jesus, Son of David." So there is no doubt of the fact that the Jews knew that the Messiah must come through David and that Jesus claimed to be the son of David.

If He were not, in fact, descended from David, it would have been a very simple thing to disprove because the Scribes and the Chief Pharisees were the keepers of the genealogical records kept near the Temple. If He were not, only a few minutes investigation could have proved that Jesus was not descended from David making him an impostor and a fraud. Considering the great expedience and lengths to which the Jews were willing to go to destroy Jesus, can anyone suppose that they had not already checked such an obvious fact as whether or not He was indeed the descendent of David?

There is not the least hint anywhere in the Gospels or the New Testament that Jesus' claim as descendent of David was ever so much as challenged. Nor is there any such charge in the first century from any other antagonist of Christianity. Keep in mind that though the Messiah must descend from David, since the destruction of the Temple and the records no Jew today could prove himself to be the descendent of David. Therefore, the Jewish Messiah had to be born before 70 A.D., when the temple and the record house were destroyed.

CONTRADICTIONS IN THE GENEALOGIES?

Let us consider some of the problems that are attendant upon these genealogies. As people have compared the two lists, the one in Matthew and the one in Luke, they have seen what would appear to be contradictions. There are vast differences in the names which are included in these genealogies, and yet they seem to be, in both cases, the genealogies of Joseph, the stepfather of Jesus. Many people have wrestled with these problems and tried to solve them. The solution is very simple when the key is seen: In Matthew we have the genealogy of Joseph (His legal lineage); in Luke we have the genealogy of Mary (His biological lineage).

Let us consider this verse in Matthew 1:16. "And Jacob begot Joseph the husband of Mary, of whom was born Jesus who is called Christ." Here Matthew is using a periphrasis, a turning of words. The point I would have you notice is: Who is the father of Joseph? And the answer here: "Jacob begot Joseph, the husband of Mary, from whom was born Jesus...." The father of Joseph is Jacob.

Let us now consider the text in Luke 3:23: "Now Jesus Himself began His ministry at about thirty years of age, being (as was supposed) the son of Joseph, the son of Heli." Here we are told that Joseph was the son of Heli. Unless Joseph had two different fathers—which is extremely difficult to do—then we see that we do not have in both cases the genealogy of Joseph. Why is it listed this way?

The Jews did not include the names of women in their genealogies. This points to another remarkable fact of this genealogy—that the names of four women are included: Tamar, Rahab, and Bathsheba, who have moral spots upon their escutcheons, and Ruth, an alien [Gentile]. In the inclusion of these women's names, God is showing us that He was willing to receive sinners and even aliens and strangers from the covenant into the grace of Jesus Christ.

Bible scholars McClintock & Strong, in their *Biblical Encyclopedia*, point out that when the blood of the grandfather passed to a grandson through a daughter, the name of the daughter was omitted and the daughter's husband was counted as the son of the grandfather. So we see that Jacob was the father of Joseph and from that came Jesus, though he was but His stepfather. Heli was the father of Mary, who was the mother of Jesus. But Joseph is counted as the son of both Jacob and Heli. In one case he was the son; in the other case he was the son-in-law.

One writer argued, "Now that cannot be because the Bible does not use that kind of language." Does it not? If you were to examine the first chapter of Ruth, you will find there that Naomi referred to Ruth as "my daughter." Was Ruth her daughter? No. She was her daughter-in-law. In 1 Samuel 24, Saul refers to David as "my son, David." Was David Saul's son? No. David was married to Michal, the daughter of Saul. He was his son-in-law, but he is called his son. This was according to the custom of the Jews.

So we see that the problem is solved when we understand that Matthew gives the genealogy of Joseph and Luke gives the genealogy of Mary. This should not be thought strange because it is very clear in the first two chapters of Matthew that Matthew is giving Joseph's story. In fact, he refers to Joseph 28 times. In the first two chapters of Luke, Luke refers to Mary scores of times. He relates Mary's song. So it is only natural that he would give the genealogy of Mary.

Furthermore, if we had two genealogies of Joseph, who was not in any way the real father of Jesus, would it not be strange for there to be no listing of His real parentage at all? In fact, it is interesting also that the Jews, according again to McClintock & Strong, called Mary in Hebrew *Bath Heli* which is "daughter of Eli." That she was, indeed, the daughter of Heli, and Joseph, her husband, was counted as his son. So that problem is resolved very beautifully in Scripture.

Another verse, perhaps even less understood than this, is

Matthew 1:12: "And after they were brought to Babylon, Jeconiah begot Shealtiel, and Shealtiel begot Zerubbabel." So we find injected in this list of descendents of David through Solomon, one Jeconiah (or *Jechonias*, in Greek). What is the problem? The problem is that in Jeremiah, we are told that Jeconiah, whose name was, in fact, "Coniah," ("Je" is simply a reference to Jehovah, often appended to Jewish names) was a wicked king. The Bible says, "Write this man down as childless ... For none of his descendants shall prosper, sitting on the throne of David" (Jeremiah 22:30).

So a roadblock is established prohibiting any seed of Jeconiah from ever having the throne of David. Yet, it is through David and through his regal line, Solomon, which goes down to Jeconiah, that the Messiah must come. Here we have an apparently insoluble mystery.

But do a little detective work with me, and you will see how the "greater-than-Houdini," who provided this lock, is the One who can provide the combination to open it. Again, let me show you the problem. The Messiah must come through David and through David's son, Solomon. But when we come down to Jeconiah, there is a cut-off and no seed of Jeconiah can ever sit upon the throne. How is the problem solved? It is solved through the lineage of Mary. It was only through Mary that the seed came to Jesus. We find that Mary's lineage goes back to David, but she does not go through Solomon; she goes through Nathan and comes around Jeconiah. Therefore, the seed of Jeconiah was not in Jesus. But the legal title to the throne came through Joseph, whereas the biological seed came around Jeconiah and did not enter into Jesus. No other couple who ever lived could have fulfilled that amazing requirement and unlocked that lock.

If Jesus had not been virgin-born, and if the seed of Joseph were in Him, He would be incapacitated to have been the Messiah because He would have been of the seed of Jeconiah. No one else could possibly have done this. It was only through David and Solomon and down through Jeconiah that He could have had the legal title to the throne. Only through Mary and Joseph, both related to David, was that prophecy able to be fulfilled—one going around the banned seed of Jeconiah; one providing the seed for Christ.

Christ will reign on David's throne. Christ will be the Branch from Jesse, upon whom God's Spirit will rest. He will usher in the Messianic age.

In addition to showing that He came of the seed of Abraham, and that He was of the tribe of Judah, it also proves that He was David's son. This was very important because, as we have seen, there are many prophecies in the Old Testament that point to the fact that Messiah must be David's son.

As mentioned before, there is not the least hint anywhere in the Gospels or the New Testament that His claim as descendent of David was ever even so much as challenged. Nor is there any charge in the first century from any other antagonist of Christianity that that was not the case. Keep in mind that though the Messiah must descend from David, since the destruction of the temple and the records, no Jew today could prove himself to be the descendent of David. Where, then, could a Messiah come from now?

CONCLUSION

So we see that the genealogical records prove that Jesus is of the seed of Abraham, He is of the tribe of Judah, and He is David's greater Son. Just by being born into this family, He fulfilled many prophecies at once.

CHAPTER 33

The Healer

❦

PROPHECY:

*Say to those who are fearful-hearted, "Be strong, do not fear. Behold,
your God will come with vengeance, with the recompense of God; He
will come and save you. Then the eyes of the blind shall be opened,
and the ears of the deaf shall be unstopped. Then the lame shall leap
like a deer, and the tongue of the dumb sing. For waters shall burst
forth in the wilderness, and streams in the desert."*
Isaiah 35:4-6

FULFILLMENT:

*Jesus answered and said to them, "Go and tell John the things which
you hear and see: The blind see and the lame walk; the lepers are
cleansed and the deaf hear; the dead are raised up and the poor have
the gospel preached to them."*
Matthew 11:4-5

As noted, John the Baptist was God's forerunner to Jesus. He
proclaimed the need for Israel to repent, to get ready for the Messiah
to come. Jesus finally came and John baptized Him. Later, because
of John's boldness in declaring that sin was sin, Herod had him im-

Jesus Healing the Sick

prisoned and eventually, beheaded. While he was in prison, he began to be unsure if Jesus really was the One to come, after all. So he sent some of his disciples to ask Jesus if He really was the Messiah. Jesus' answer is recounted above.

What was Jesus' response to John's doubts? Jesus sent word back to him that He was healing the sick and the lame and the blind.

Jesus was pointing out to John how His life was fulfilling that which was prophesied in Isaiah 35.

Jesus Christ, the healer, brought delight to many. Listen to how bestselling author and speaker Max Lucado puts it:

> Delight is the look on Andrew's face at the lunch pail that never came up empty. Delight is the dozing guests who drank the wine that had been water. Delight is Jesus walking through waves as casually as you walk through curtains. Delight is a leper seeing a finger where there had been only a nub ... a widow hosting a party with food made for a funeral ... a paraplegic doing somersaults. Delight is Jesus doing impossible things in crazy ways: healing the blind with spit, paying taxes with a coin found in a fish's mouth, and coming back from the dead disguised as a gardener.[47]

Jesus, the healer, brought new life and joy to everyone whose life He touched.

THERAPY

In the Gospels we read that Jesus Christ went about healing the sick. He laid hands on people, and they got well. Christ's teaching message was made tangible by His healing ministry. Each healing was an eloquent sermon that made the point that He was Lord, even over sickness and death. The Greek word for "to heal" is *therapeo*, from which we get the word therapy. Therapy is healing. And no one healed like Jesus Christ. Once word got out about His healing powers, He could not even move about freely because everyone brought their sick to Him. Through His healing, He was announcing to the whole world that the Messiah had come.

Bible commentator Matthew Henry shows just how special these miracles of healing Jesus did were:

Wonders shall be wrought in the kingdoms both of nature and grace, wonders of mercy wrought upon the children of men, sufficient to evince that it is no less than a God that comes to us.... Wonders shall be wrought on men's bodies (v. 5, 6): *The eyes of the blind shall be opened*; this was often done by our Lord Jesus when he was here upon earth, with a word's speaking, and one he gave sight to that was *born* blind, Matthew ix. 27; xii. 22; xx. 30; John ix. 6. By his power the ears of the deaf also were unstopped, with one word. *Ephphatha—Be opened*, Mark vii. 34. Many that were lame had the use of their limbs restored so perfectly that they could not only go, but *leap*, and with so much joy to them that they could not forbear leaping for joy, as that impotent man, Acts iii. 8. The dumb also were enabled to speak, and then no marvel that they were disposed to sing for joy, Matthew ix. 32, 33.[48]

Both the people (the *hoi polloi*) and the temple authorities recognized that Jesus was doing special miracles. His enemies even attributed His miraculous works to sorcery, but this shows that they acknowledged He was doing supernatural things—they were just attributing the power to the wrong source. Henry continues:

These miracles Christ wrought to prove that he was sent of God (John iii. 2), nay, working them by his own power and in his own name, he proved that he was God, the same who at first made man's mouth, the hearing ear, and the seeing eye. When he would prove to John's disciples his divine mission he did it by miracles of this kind, in which this scripture was fulfilled...Wonders, greater wonders, shall be wrought on men's souls. By the word and Spirit of Christ those that were spiritually blind were enlightened (Acts xxvi. 18), those that were deaf to the calls of God were made to hear them readily, so Lydia, whose heart *the Lord opened*, so *that she attended*, Acts xvi. 14. Those that were impotent to every thing that is good by divine grace are made, not only able for it, but active in it, and run the way of God's commandments. Those also that were dumb, and knew not how to speak of God or to God, having their understandings opened to know him, shall thereby have their lips opened to show forth his praise. The tongue of the dumb shall sing for joy, the joy of God's salvation. Praise shall be perfected out of the mouth of babes and sucklings.[49]

CONCLUSION

The miracles of Jesus were enacted parables. For example, Jesus is the light of the world and He provided light for the blind. The miracles were proof enough for John the Baptist, and should be proof enough for us. These miracles, too, like virtually everything in the life of Jesus, were foretold.

CHAPTER 34

A Voice Crying in the Wilderness

❦

PROPHECY:

The voice of one crying in the wilderness: "Prepare the way of the Lord; make straight in the desert a highway for our God. Every valley shall be exalted and every mountain and hill brought low; the crooked places shall be made straight and the rough places smooth; the glory of the Lord shall be revealed, and all flesh shall see it together; for the mouth of the Lord has spoken."
Isaiah 40:3–5

FULFILLMENT:

[W]hile Annas and Caiaphas were high priests, the word of God came to John the son of Zacharias in the wilderness. And he went into all the region around the Jordan, preaching a baptism of repentance for the remission of sins, as it is written in the book of the words of Isaiah the prophet, saying: "The voice of one crying in the wilderness: 'Prepare the way of the Lord; make His paths straight.'"
Luke 3:2–4

Can you imagine the amount of work involved in preparing the ground for a new highway? Old tree stumps must be uprooted, rivers and streams diverted, tunnels channeled through rocky mountain interiors, and all the underbrush cleared away. Because it is worthwhile, the project continues until the job is done.

According to Old Testament prophets, before the Messiah would appear, a special messenger would make every effort to clear the spiritual debris from the path of the anointed King. He would come in the power and spirit of Elijah the prophet. (In the last book of the Old Testament, Malachi, it is written that Elijah would come.) He would turn the hearts of Israel back to God and prepare them to recognize the true Messiah.

These prophecies were fulfilled by John the Baptist (Matthew 11:13–14). He came as a prophet to proclaim God's Word and call the nation of Israel to repentance. As a Nazirite, he was set apart by God as a special witness, and gave himself completely to God's calling in his life (Numbers 6:2–3; Luke 1:15).

Once John realized, through the inspiration of the Holy Spirit and a public pronouncement from Heaven (Matthew 3:13–17), that Jesus was the promised Messiah—the Son of the Living God—he proclaimed without reservation that "He who believes in the Son has everlasting life; and he who does not believe the Son shall not see life, but the wrath of God abides on him" (John 3:36).

However, when imprisoned and facing death, he wondered if Jesus truly did fulfill the Old Testament prophecies. His new doubts sprang from the common misconception that the Messiah would be a political deliverer. Yet, even in the midst of his doubts, John sought answers to his questions from Jesus himself, demonstrating his continued acceptance and trust in Christ's divine authority (Matthew 11:1–4).

CONCLUSION

John stood firm in his confession of Christ and of the need for repentance, even in the face of government pressure and the plots

John the Baptist Preaching in the Wilderness

of religious hypocrites (Mark 6:17–18; Luke 3:7–14). This man of God is an excellent example of the type of messenger we should attempt to be, as we strive to give a faithful witness of Christ. Like John, when confronted with doubts, we need to seek out Jesus for our answers.

231

CHAPTER 35

The Smitten One

☙❧

PROPHECY:

I gave My back to those who struck Me, and My cheeks to those who plucked out the beard; I did not hide My face from shame and spitting.
Isaiah 50:6

"And I will pour on the house of David and on the inhabitants of Jerusalem the Spirit of grace and supplication; then they will look on Me whom they pierced. Yes, they will mourn for Him as one mourns for his only son, and grieve for Him as one grieves for a firstborn."
Zechariah 12:10

FULFILLMENT:

Then they spat in His face and beat Him; and others struck Him with the palms of their hands.... and when he had scourged Jesus, he delivered Him to be crucified.
Matthew 26:67; 27:26

Then He said to Thomas, "Reach your finger here, and look at My hands; and reach your hand here, and put it into My side. Do not be unbelieving, but believing."
John 20:27

Many times we forget the very real physical suffering and torture Christ was subjected to before His crucifixion. He was whipped 39 times with a cat-o'-nine-tails until His back was a bloody pulp of torn flesh and blood. The Roman guards made sport of Him, beating His face, tearing away His beard, and hitting Him with clubs. They mocked, stripped, and humiliated Him.

Biblical apologist Mike Licona has written some books on the resurrection of Jesus. Co-author Jerry Newcombe asked his opinion of Mel Gibson's movie, *The Passion of the Christ:*

> I thought *The Passion* was a very accurate portrayal of the last few hours of Jesus' life; in particular, the portrayal of Jesus' scourging, I think, was very noteworthy. Scourging was a brutal practice. The first century Jewish historian Josephus referred to a man who had been filleted to the bone with whips. And a second century text referred to as *The Martyrdom of Polycarp*, mentions how the Roman whips were able to expose veins and arteries. So, it was a horrible practice.[50]

Of course, the scourging was a prelude to the crucifixion.

During this entire time, Christ had the power to free Himself, destroy the Roman guards, and bring God's wrath upon Jerusalem. Yet, He held back the divine retribution and suffered for the redemption of His people. Nothing speaks so loudly of God's love as Jesus' acceptance of man's sinful abuse.

The Jewish nation and the Jewish religion have rejected Jesus as the chosen Messiah. Yet, God prophesies through Zechariah of a day in which He will reach out to the Jewish people in a spirit of grace and open their eyes to the truth. They then will weep and grieve over their rejection of the true Messiah. Large numbers of them will accept Jesus and trust in Him as their personal Lord and Savior and thus become part of the "New Israel"—the Church

(Romans 11).

CONCLUSION

We must never forget the suffering Christ endured for our salvation. Knowledge of it should inspire each of us to fully dedicate ourselves to God's will for our lives (John 17:1–5). It should compel us to give all we have to the service of God our King.

Let's explore His suffering for us even further.

CHAPTER 36

A Suffering King

PROPHECY:

But He was wounded for our transgressions, He was bruised for our iniquities; The chastisement for our peace was upon Him, and by His stripes we are healed. ... He was oppressed and He was afflicted, yet He opened not His mouth; He was led as a lamb to the slaughter, and as a sheep before its shearers is silent, so He opened not His mouth. ... And they made His grave with the wicked—but with the rich at His death, because He had done no violence, nor was any deceit in His mouth. ... Therefore I will divide Him a portion with the great, and He shall divide the spoil with the strong, because He poured out His soul unto death, and He was numbered with the transgressors.
Isaiah 53:5,7,9,12

FULFILLMENT:

"For even the Son of Man did not come to be served, but to serve, and to give His life a ransom for many...." Then Pilate asked Him again, saying, "Do You answer nothing? See how many things they testify against You!" But Jesus still answered nothing, so that Pilate marveled.... With Him they also crucified two robbers, one on His right and the other on His left. So the Scripture was fulfilled which says, "And He was numbered with the transgressors."
Mark 10:45; 15:4–5, 27–28

Now when evening had come, there came a rich man from Arimathea, named Joseph, who himself had also become a disciple of Jesus.... and laid it [Christ's body] in his new tomb which he had hewn out of the rock; and he rolled a large stone against the door of the tomb, and departed."
Matthew 27:57, 60

Isaiah 53 is such a critical chapter of Scripture that we will deal with it in two parts. This first chapter will provide a quick overview, namely that Jesus (at His first coming) was the foretold suffering servant, not the conquering king. In the next chapter, we will unpack some of the incredible prophecies in Isaiah 53, verse by verse.

WHEN WE THINK OF A KING

When we think of a king, our minds conjure up images of riches, palaces, feasts, and comfort. A king is one who has hundreds of servants and every possible convenience. Yet, in the fifty-third chapter of Isaiah, the prophet paints a startlingly different picture of God's coming King. He predicts that the Messiah would come to be a servant, committed to dying for the sins of His people.

This passage, which foretells the suffering of Christ, teaches the atoning work the Messiah would accomplish by His death. The prophecy is so detailed that any objective reader would quickly identify the promised suffering servant as Jesus.

I know this to be true because I once asked a Jewish friend to listen to a passage of Scripture and to tell me whom he thought it identified. I read the entire fifty-third chapter of Isaiah without telling him the text. When I had finished reading, he responded instantly, "I don't believe in the New Testament." I then showed him that I was reading the words of the Jewish prophet Isaiah from the Old Testament. Indeed, no unbiased reader would fail to recognize

Jesus as the fulfillment of this Old Testament Messianic prophecy.

The concrete details of the Messiah's suffering that are set forth in Isaiah 53 are of the greatest significance. Isaiah points out that the Christ would not attempt to defend Himself before His accusers, but would voluntarily give His life as a sacrifice. This Jesus did, to the amazement of Pilate, who could not understand how any man facing the torturous death of crucifixion would fail to plead for his own life.

This passage also proclaims the substitutionary work of Jesus' death on the Cross. He has borne our sorrows and our griefs; He was smitten by God, wounded for our transgressions, bruised for our iniquities. The punishment of our sins was placed upon Him so that we might have peace with God (Isaiah 53:4–6).

God indicates by this Old Testament picture of His "suffering servant" that the promised Messiah was not simply called to rule with a fist of iron, but that He was also sent as Redeemer and Savior. God's chosen Servant would rule, but only after He had suffered for the sins of God's people and had been exalted by God (Isaiah 53:10–12).

CONCLUSION

Jesus is the only historical figure who fulfills all the details of this prophecy. Isaiah 53 makes it clear that Jesus of Nazareth is the chosen Savior of men (Acts 8:27–40). We have more to say on this marvelous chapter of Isaiah 53 in the next chapter.

CHAPTER 37

The New Testament in the Old

꩜

PROPHECY:
And I will put enmity between you and the woman, and between
your seed and her Seed; He shall bruise your head,
and you shall bruise His heel.
Genesis 3:15

FULFILLMENT:
He who sins is of the devil, for the devil has sinned from the
beginning. For this purpose the Son of God was manifested,
that He might destroy the works of the devil.
1 John 3:8

Chapter 53 of Isaiah is, in my opinion, and that of many others, the most astonishing chapter in all of Holy Scripture. In fact, I would say it is the most astonishing piece of writing in all of history. There is nothing like it whatsoever. It is as if a passage from the New Testament were directly transplanted into the Old Testament.

This passage is worth repeating *in toto*:

¹ Who has believed our report?

And to whom has the arm of the LORD been
revealed?
²For He shall grow up before Him as a tender
plant,
And as a root out of dry ground.
He has no form or comeliness;
And when we see Him,
There is no beauty that we should desire Him.
³He is despised and rejected by men,
A Man of sorrows and acquainted with grief.
And we hid, as it were, our faces from Him;
He was despised, and we did not esteem Him.
⁴Surely He has borne our griefs
And carried our sorrows;
Yet we esteemed Him stricken,
Smitten by God, and afflicted.
⁵But He was wounded for our transgressions,
He was bruised for our iniquities;
The chastisement for our peace was upon Him,
And by His stripes we are Healed.
⁶All we like sheep have gone astray;
We have turned, every one, to his own way;
And the LORD has laid on Him the iniquity of
us all.
⁷He was oppressed and He was afflicted,
Yet He opened not His mouth;
He was led as a lamb to the slaughter,
And as a sheep before its shearers is silent,
So He opened not His mouth.
⁸He was taken from prison and from judgment,
And who will declare His generation?
For He was cut off from the land of the living;
For the transgressions of My people He was
stricken.

9And they made His grave with the wicked—
But with the rich at His death,
Because He had done no violence,
Nor was any deceit in His mouth.
10Yet it pleased the LORD to bruise Him;
He has put Him to grief.
When You make His soul an offering for sin,
He shall see His seed, He shall prolong His days,
And the pleasure of the LORD shall prosper in
His hand.
11He shall see the labor of His soul, and be
satisfied.
By His knowledge My righteous Servant shall
justify many,
For He shall bear their iniquities.
12Therefore I will divide Him a portion with
the great,
And He shall divide the spoil with the strong,
Because He poured out His soul unto death,
And He was numbered with the transgressors,
And He bore the sin of many,
And made intercession for the transgressors.

Isaiah 53 was written over 700 years before Jesus Christ was born, and yet here is laid out in great detail the life, the ministry, the suffering, the death, and the resurrection of Jesus Christ. There is nothing like this in any other religious writing. It is unique in the truest sense of that word. It is truly remarkable. It obviously proves that the Scriptures are inspired by God. There is no other explanation under which such a thing could exist.

And there is no way it can be said that it was written after Christ was born. I have seen the actual manuscript taken from the Dead Sea Scrolls, written before Christ was born. Furthermore, in 300 B.C., in the Septuagint translation, the Old Testament was translated into

Greek and spread around the world. It would have been impossible to insert anything. This was, indeed, written seven centuries before Christ was born.

"Who has believed our report? And to whom has the arm of the LORD been revealed? For He shall grow up before Him as a tender plant, and as a root out of dry ground" (Isaiah 53:1-2). And so Christ came—not with pomp and circumstance, not with royalty, not with power, not with armies—but in a poor family with a great lineage that had fallen into poverty. He grew up in the home of a carpenter. He grew up in a city that was a byword: "Can anything good come out of Nazareth?" (John 1:46). He grew up with no education, having never learned in any official school, and yet He was the wisest person who ever lived. He grew up astonishingly. He exited that town, which was nothing, walked up on a hill, with no background, no education, and delivered the greatest discourse on human ethics the world has ever heard. It has never been equaled and certainly never excelled—the Sermon on the Mount.

But because He did not come with grandeur and pomp and power, because He did not come as a reigning general to overthrow the Roman Empire, He was rejected. He was despised of men, and His entire life was that of a Man of Sorrows and a man acquainted with grief. It is never once recorded that Jesus ever laughed, and yet the night before He went to the agony of the Cross, He said, "These things I have spoken to you, that My joy may remain in you" (John 15:11). He came from the source of all joy—from Heaven—and He came to bring that joy to us, but He took all of our sorrows and our griefs upon Himself. Thus, He never laughed. He did weep, and He wept only for us.

He was despised and rejected of men, and that is still true to this day. If you go into any Islamic country, Mohammed's name is highly prized. If you go into the lands of the religion of Buddha, His name is reverenced, but here in Christian America, the name of Christ is despised. Only Christ. He said of Himself that "[t]hey hated Me without a cause" (John 15:25).

What has He done? I have wanted to say to the next person I hear blaspheme His name, "Why do you take His name in blasphemy? What has He done to you? He loved you. He desires that you might be forgiven and receive eternal life. He has done naught but good for this world. Why do you hate Him so?"

The only answer to that is the depravity of the hearts of men, and His is that one name which, if the world could do it, would be stamped out forever. It is now continually being removed from the public square, where efforts are often made to forbid the mention of His name in public meetings. This has been true in schools and all sorts of other organizations. He is rejected of men.

"Surely He has borne our griefs and carried our sorrows; yet we esteemed Him stricken, smitten by God, and afflicted" (Isaiah 53:4). They did everything imaginable to him. They spat in His face; they ripped off his beard; they scourged Him with a gruesome implement.

Now the Jews limited their scourging to forty stripes minus one, but the Romans had no such compunctions. It is estimated that He received more than one hundred blows with the scourge. There was hardly a spot on His body that had not been ripped opened, because you see, Pilate did not intend that scourging would be what it usually is—a prelude to crucifixion. Otherwise, the person would never be able to get to the cross. Pilate intended that Jesus merely be scourged, as awful as that was: "I will scourge Him and let Him go," he said.

And so, the soldiers gave Him what they felt was almost equal to crucifixion—a substitute. But when they brought Him back and said, "Behold the man," the temple authorities were not satisfied, and they cried out, "Let Him be crucified" (John 19:5-6). And so it became not a substitute, but a prelude to crucifixion. Indeed, His form was more marred than that of any man, and that was done for us.

He was smitten by God. He endured the nails pounded into hands and feet, the crown of thorns, the agony of the Cross, but all

The Crucifixion

of this was just a prelude to an even greater punishment—the punishment of His Father. He was smitten of God and afflicted. We are told, "Yet it pleased the LORD to bruise Him; He has put Him to grief" (Isaiah 53:10). And this was His only and beloved Son, about whom He said, "This is My beloved Son, in whom I am well pleased" (Matthew 3:17). The Father had loved Him for all eternity.

Referring to His Father, Jesus said, "I always do those things that please Him" (John 8:29). And now, again, He is smitten by God. God now pours out all of His wrath for sin upon His only beloved Son.

Jesus was silent, we are told. He "opened not His mouth" before His accusers. As a lamb taken to the slaughter, He opened not His mouth. Why was Christ silent before that trial? He could have defended Himself easily. They could not prove anything against Him. He, indeed, confessed that He was the Son of God, when questioned. And this is what brought about His crucifixion.

He could easily have escaped that trial. He could have defended Himself and said, "You can see that I am not guilty of any of these charges. Which of you convicts Me of sin?" (John 8:45). There was no deceit, no lie in His mouth. He was absolutely without sin. So why did He not say something?

The reason is that He *was* guilty. He was the most guilty man the world has ever seen, for all of *our* guilt was imputed to Him, and He became *sin* for us. It was your guilt and mine that was upon Him, for which He was enduring all of this agony. He bore our griefs and carried our sorrows and had imputed to Him our guilt. He became sin (2 Corinthians 5:21).

Now we know that God loves us and we know that God loves us with an infinite love. But God hates sin, and God hates sin with an infinite hatred. Consider that. All of that wrath for sin was poured out upon Jesus Christ.

> All we like sheep have gone astray; we have turned, every one, to his own way; and the LORD has laid on Him the iniquity of us all. He was oppressed and He was afflicted, yet He opened not His mouth; He was led as a lamb to the slaughter, and as a sheep before its shearers is silent, so He opened not His mouth.

That is because He was bearing our guilt before the Judgment Seat and taking our place (Isaiah 53:6–7).

"He was taken from prison and from judgment.… He was cut off from the land of the living" (v. 8). Here we see that He had been in judgment, He had been in prison, and He was crucified and killed, but it was "for the transgressions of My people" that He was stricken. Amazing! How could anyone know any of these things about someone who would not be for several centuries?

"And they made His grave with the wicked—but with the rich at His death" (v. 9). If the governor had had his plan, as usual, and the temple authorities had had their desire, His body would have been thrown into a common grave with the other malefactors on their crosses. But God had another plan, and so He was buried in a rich man's tomb—that of Joseph of Arimathea. Here, again, is an amazing prophecy fulfilled.

In spite of the Messiah's suffering comes a statement that astounded me when I first heard it: "Yet it pleased the LORD to bruise Him; He has put Him to grief" (v. 10). That a Father could look down upon His only child, His beloved child, His perfect child, and that it would please Him to bruise Him and put Him to grief, shocked me. Of course, that "please" does not mean pleasant; it means that it was the will of God. It was the will of God that Christ come and take upon Himself human flesh. It was the will of God that sin should be imputed to Him and that He should die in our place. The alternative was that every one of us would go to Hell.

The holiness and the justice of God must be satisfied. God cannot become unjust. Sin must have its recompense. The soul that sins shall surely die (Ezekiel 18:3). So we see the travail of Christ's soul, and when the Father saw the travail of His soul, He was satisfied. The justice of God was satisfied by His knowledge, that is, "By His knowledge My righteous Servant shall justify many" (v. 11). This is salvation—to know God and to know Jesus Christ, whom He has sent. This is eternal life. We are justified by knowing Christ, knowing Him who is the Son of God, the Savior of men, knowing Him who took our sins upon Himself and died in our place. This is what causes our justification. It is through knowledge and trust in Christ, our Savior.

Then comes a new development. Who could possibly know this? That after this person has been cut off out of the land of the living, after He has endured death, we read that God will, indeed, prolong His days. Here the concept of life beyond death, a resurrection from the grave, is taught, and furthermore, that the pleasure of the Lord shall prosper in His hands. Christ does all things well, and the pleasure or the purpose of God will prosper in His hand, and it is, and it will be yet more. God is accomplishing His purpose that the Gospel of Christ would spread all over the earth, as the waters cover the sea. We are told that the knowledge of God would spread around the world, and it is doing so today.

I am amazed how few people know that we are living in the midst of the greatest ingathering into the Church in the history of mankind. In the last thirty years, since 1980, the number of converts to Christ has grown 1,000 percent—ten times. In 1980, there were 20,000 converts to Christ per day worldwide. By the late 1990s, it was estimated that the growth was over 150,000 converts a day, and it continues to grow. Some of you may live long enough to see the Gospel covering the world as has never been heard of before. You may live to see this country transformed by the power of Jesus Christ, and so many of the ills that have plagued our nation will dissolve away because the pleasure of the Lord will prosper in the hand of Him who was skewered to a Cross.

Christ does all things well, and the purpose of God that humanity would come to know the living Christ and the living God, and that the people of every tribe and nation of the world would come to know His salvation, will come to pass. Christ has guaranteed it. Therefore, God says that He will "divide the spoil with the strong, because He poured out His soul unto death." Christ will "divide the spoil with the strong;" God is willing to bless us who have faithfully followed Him.

He is the great Conqueror, not merely of the Roman Empire, but of all of the evils of this world, and we who are the soldiers of Christ can follow Him and be partakers of that spoil, whatever that phrase actually means. Christ is the great One. He is the great Conqueror, and He has done it, and we have an opportunity to share with Him in the results of that, because He has poured out His soul unto death. He was numbered with the transgressors and made intercession for the transgressors.

The New Testament is the final authority on the interpretation of the Old. Perhaps you remember the story of Philip in Acts 8, when he was out in the desert and saw the Ethiopian eunuch in a chariot and the Holy Spirit said, "Go near and overtake this chariot" (Acts 8:29). The eunuch was reading the Old Testament, which is all that was available at that time.

When Philip asked, he said that he was reading a part of Isaiah 53. Then the eunuch asked Philip a question: About whom is the writer speaking—about himself, or about some other? Beginning at that Scripture, Philip preached Jesus to him. So we see that the authoritative New Testament Scripture makes very clear that this Old Testament passage is talking about Jesus Christ. The very content makes it absolutely crystal clear.

How did that happen? Lucky guesses? Hardly. Are there any among you who have doubted that the Scriptures are the inspired Word of God? If so, explain to me how Isaiah 53 could have been written 700 years before Christ. You cannot. I know that, and in your heart, so do you.

CONCLUSION

For centuries now, Jewish synagogues and temples have generally stayed away from the public reading of Isaiah 53—for obvious reasons. The words conjure up in most people's minds the crucifixion of Jesus Christ.

Old Testament Jews knew that the Messiah would be a great high priest to offer sacrifices, but they never dreamt He would offer

Himself as a sacrifice. Today, when confronted with this prophecy from the Old Testament, a Jew is most likely to say, "Well, that suffering Savior, that righteous one, is referring to the State of Israel." My friends, that just won't wash. Any true investigation makes that very clear.

Even the greatest of the authorities on Jewish tradition and law, Maimonides, said when this idea first appeared (in about 1100 A.D.) that it is a false use of the prophecy. In other words, the great Jewish scholar said that Isaiah 53 did refer to a specific, individual Messiah. He, who is regarded as the Jews' highest authority, said that his individual view is one that had been held universally by Jews in all of the prior centuries. It is a picture of a suffering Messiah who was to come to die for us. (Of course, tragically, Maimonides did not see *Jesus* as the one fulfilling this chapter, but rather some future figure.)

CHAPTER 38

Good News for the Poor

᚛᚛

PROPHECY:

"The Spirit of the Lord God is upon Me, because the Lord has anointed Me to preach good tidings to the poor; He has sent Me to heal the brokenhearted, to proclaim liberty to the captives, and the opening of the prison to those who are bound; to proclaim the acceptable year of the Lord, and the day of vengeance of our God; to comfort all who mourn...."
Isaiah 61:1–2

FULFILLMENT:

"The Spirit of the Lord is upon Me, because He has anointed Me to preach the gospel to the poor; He has sent Me to heal the brokenhearted, to proclaim liberty to the captives and recovery of sight to the blind, to set at liberty those who are oppressed; to proclaim the acceptable year of the Lord."... And He began to say to them, "Today this Scripture is fulfilled in your hearing."
Luke 4:18–19, 21

Why did Jesus come? As we saw in the last chapter, Isaiah tells us that He came to bear our sorrows. Jesus came to be struck down by God and afflicted on our behalf. He was wounded and bruised because of our sins. We have all gone astray, but God the Father chose to use the horrible passion of His Son as the means of forgiveness (Isaiah 53:4-6). He came to offer a sacrifice. This passage sums up the message of the whole Bible. The entire revelation from beginning to end has various themes and sub-themes, but this theme—the death of Jesus for our sins and His resurrection—is the very heart and soul of the Bible.

He came to proclaim Good News to those that need it beginning with the Good News that He took upon Himself our sin.

The great Christian historian, Dr. Paul L. Maier, wrote the book, *In The Fullness of Time*, about how God sent His Son at just the right time in history. In reference to this passage in Luke's Gospel (from Isaiah), Dr. Maier writes:

> It was an astounding event that Sabbath day when the widow Mary's Son stood up in the Nazareth synagogue to read from the scroll of the prophet Isaiah. Yeshua (later Hellenized to "Jesus") was a little over thirty years old, this carpenter who not long before had submitted to a sacred washing called baptism at the hands of his cousin John. Jesus had survived a lonely spiritual contest with Evil in the desert, but now prepared to go public with the words of his favorite prophet:
>
> "The Spirit of the LORD is upon me, because he has anointed me to preach good news to the poor. He has sent me to proclaim release to the captives and recovery of sight to the blind, to let the oppressed go free, to proclaim the year of the LORD's favor" (Luke 4:18).
>
> Jesus closed the scroll, handed it back to the at-

tendant, and then declared, in syllables stupendous with significance, *"Today this scripture has been fulfilled in your hearing."*

The worshipers were awestruck: only the Messiah could make such a claim. It was an appropriate beginning for Jesus' ministry, since the rest of it would only enlarge on that statement in word and deed. His family was shocked, particularly his four half-brothers and two half-sisters, who even debated his sanity. Only later, after the resurrection, would they fully convert to his cause.[51]

This is very well put.

THE MINISTRY BEGINS

In this passage, Isaiah depicts the Christ as a minister to those who are oppressed by society. In His first sermon, Jesus identified Himself as the long awaited "healer of the brokenhearted." Even those who deny His divinity recognize that Jesus was always ministering to the outcasts of society: healing the sick, feeding the poor, and redeeming sinners.

Yet, in a deeper sense, this prophecy is speaking of the spiritually poor, spiritually imprisoned, spiritually bound, spiritually blind, and spiritually bruised (Matthew 5:1–12). An even more detailed examination reveals that our lives are fertile ground for this ministry of Christ.

Spiritual poverty is a universal condition that no government can alleviate. Only Christ can cancel our spiritual debt. However, we cannot come to Him for assistance if we are proud of our own good works and confident that we have thus earned a ticket to eternity in Heaven. Jesus told a parable about a Pharisee who thanked God that he was so much more righteous than other men while beside him a tax collector beat his breast and said, "God, be merciful to me a sinner." Jesus said that the tax collector "went down to his

The Tax Collector and the Pharisee

house justified rather than the other; for everyone who exalts himself will be humbled, and he who humbles himself will be exalted" (Luke 18:14).

If we do not see how completely we have missed God's perfect standard of holiness, we also will fail to enjoy God's eternal salvation. Only those who admit their own lack of righteousness can be made rich by Christ's abundant grace. We must admit our complete need of a Savior before we will see in Jesus Christ the answer to our desperate need.

Not only must we recognize that we are spiritually poor, but also that our iniquities have condemned and imprisoned us with the just wrath of God. In our natural state, we are spiritually dead. But Christ, in His grace, has taken our punishment upon Himself by paying the full price. He alone has the right and the power to free us from our death sentence. The verdict of "not guilty" is handed down to us from God on the basis of Christ's work on our behalf (Isaiah 53).

In our natural state, we are also totally bound by the power of sin. We are incapable of doing good. Our very nature is imprisoned by infatuation with sin. Though sin manifests itself in different disguises—sometimes in open depravity, sometimes in religious hypocrisy and legalism—nevertheless, we are bound by it and unable to change our hearts to conform to God's law (Romans 8:7–8). Only Christ's sovereign grace can break the chains of sin. Powerless to free ourselves, He alone can renew our hearts and liberate us.

Another affliction that Christ came to cure is our spiritual blindness. Sin has not only affected our will, but has also affected our ability to perceive our world and ourselves as they really are. We are unable to view religion and philosophy objectively because we are innately prejudiced against the God of the Bible. Blind to God's truth, we stumble—basing our religious dogma and philosophies on our own insights, rather than on God's revelation. Only Christ can heal our blindness and allow our minds to see God, ourselves, and our world in the proper light (Revelation 3:14–22).

Our transgressions have also "bruised" our lives. Our sin has scarred us psychologically, emotionally, and spiritually. Each of us has been battered by the effects of sin: Teenagers who have given in to the temptation of cheap sex or drugs are left feeling alone and used; parents who abuse their own children experience the agony of grief and guilt; businessmen and women who neglect their families and find themselves addicted to both work and alcohol feel helpless and unfulfilled. All are victims of their own sins—all suffer the internal destruction that results from disobeying God and His law.

Because of our sins and the effects they have on us, we find ourselves at times unable to cope. We recognize that something is destroying us, something is poisoning our lives, but we cannot put our finger on it. We cannot heal ourselves.

God has told us the source of our distress. Sin is the poison contaminating our lives. No one can escape the pain that sin causes. Yet, Christ came to heal us of these "bruises." He comforts us and forgives us and gives us a new life in Him (2 Corinthians 5:17). He is the great physician and puts upon our wounds the healing balm of His mercy, which restores our spiritual health (Psalm 23). He extracts the poisonous venom of sin and replaces it with the lifegiving power of His Spirit. Jesus is greater than our sins and grants us hope in the midst of our despair and pain.

The Messiah is, indeed, the healer and liberator of the ages. The clarity with which Isaiah reveals our Lord's nature and purpose is only surpassed by the reality of Christ's redeeming touch in our lives.

ETERNAL BLISS

The Bible tells us that we are all sinful. In fact, Isaiah even said that our so-called righteous deeds (apart from God's mercy) are filthy rags before the holy God. Everything we do is tainted. Even supposedly good deeds are often done for the reciprocal effects. Isaiah writes: "But we are all like an unclean thing, and all our righteousnesses are like filthy rags; we all fade as a leaf, and our iniquities, like the wind, have taken us away" (Isaiah 64:6).

Where is the way to God to be found? Isaiah 35:10 says, "And the ransomed of the LORD shall return, and come to Zion with singing, with everlasting joy on their heads. They shall obtain joy and gladness, and sorrow and sighing shall flee away" (Isaiah 35:10). God is the one who satisfies the thirst of the thirsty and meets the desires of the heart. He provides a way that fills human hearts with joy. That is what people really want in life. They want joy. But most people, I am afraid, never find that joy. When we are finally home, this prophecy will also be true in a physical sense. The blind will see, all physical problems and all pain will be over, and Isaiah's prophecy will see its final fulfillment.

Though it is true that there is sorrow and sighing even among those who travel on the highway to Heaven, they, too, are human and are subject to all of the pains and losses of this world. The death of loved ones, the betrayal of friends, the pain and suffering of sickness and accident—all of those things befall the good and the evil, the saved and the lost. But there is a vast difference, because we are told that the sorrow and sighing shall flee away and that everlasting gladness shall descend upon our head.

With the unbeliever, though there may be moments of mirth and laughter, there is a continual heaviness and darkness and sorrow in their lives. Do not take my word for it. Listen to their own testimony.

- The famous Voltaire—a more famous skeptic could not be imagined—said, "I wish that I had never been born."
- Millionaire Jay Gould, who had it all, said, "I suppose I am the most miserable man on earth."
- Lord Byron, though he had every imaginable fame and honor bestowed upon him, including nobility, was an unbeliever who did not have Christ. Did he have joy? Does the world give true joy and true happiness? He said, "The worm, the canker and the grief are mine alone."
- The noted Disraeli, prime minister of England, said, "Youth is a mistake; manhood a struggle; old age a regret."

Such testimonies could be multiplied almost unendingly demonstrating how Satan deceives the world into thinking people will find joy in earthly things, apart from God—that God is some cosmic tyrant who is bent on making them miserable when, in fact, the very opposite is the truth. There is joy in serving Jesus.

In our stead, Jesus suffered the bitter penalty of sin until at last He could cry out, "It is finished." It is done. It is paid. *Tetelestai.* (*Tetelestai* is the Greek word used in the New Testament where Jesus says, "It is finished." It means that the debt was paid in full.) Jesus paid a price on the Cross that He did not owe—a price that we could never pay. Now, having risen from the dead, He offers us the gift of everlasting life.

How tragic it is that any should perish and lose their soul, when everlasting life is offered freely. If we were told that we must climb Mount Everest to obtain the eternal salvation of our soul, millions would attempt it, but many would not be able. We are told that it is absolutely free, that it was paid for by another at an infinite cost, and that it may be ours—if we will place our trust in Christ, if we will place our hope in Him, if we will invite Him into our lives, if we will surrender ourselves in repentance to His saviorhood and lordship.

THE NARROW ROAD

If you have never accepted Jesus Christ as your Savior and Lord, please pray along these lines: "Lord Jesus Christ, You are the way and you are the goal, but even more, You are the door that leads to the way. I enter through your Cross right now and embrace You as Savior and Lord, Who alone can give meaning to this life and hope in the midst of pain and sorrow and the promise of everlasting joy."

If you prayed that prayer in sincerity, you have begun the greatest adventure on which you could ever embark. I would strongly urge you to begin to read the Bible every day and to pray. If you have never read the Bible before, please start with the Gospel of John (the fourth book of the New Testament).

I also urge you to get involved in a Bible-based, Bible-believing church. If you would like a free book to help you become established in the Christian faith, write to Coral Ridge Ministries and ask for the book, *Beginning Again.*[52]

Once we know Jesus as our personal Lord and Savior, our "thank you" to Him for His gift of salvation will be to serve Him in every area of our life. Good works will naturally flow from our lives, as good apples grow naturally on a good apple tree.

It is one thing to know *about* Jesus the Anointed One sent by God the Father. It is another thing to *know* Jesus Christ personally. If you sincerely said that prayer, then you are on the path which leads to everlasting joy, walking with the Anointed One and living your life from henceforth for Him and for His glory. May God bless you in this new venture.

THE MAN ON THE WHITE HORSE

In this book, we have seen Him, God's Messiah, the Anointed One. We have seen Him coming to earth in humility, born in a simple stable. We have seen Him rejected and suffering as the final sacrifice. But this is not all there is, for John shows us the glory of the conquering King:

> Now I saw heaven opened, and behold, a white horse. And He who sat on him was called Faithful and True, and in righteousness He judges and makes war. His eyes were like a flame of fire, and on His head were many crowns....He has on His robe and on His thigh a name written:
>
> KING OF KINGS AND LORD OF LORDS (Revelation 19:11-12, 16).

This is the Messiah, whose first coming we have attempted to explore in depth in this present volume. Meanwhile, all of history marches toward its climax, His second coming.

Even so, come quickly, Lord Jesus. Amen.

Soli Deo Gloria.

Acknowledgments

There are numerous people to thank for their contributions to this book. First, thanks to Donald E. Van Curler, who made the whole project possible. Special thanks go to Kirsti Newcombe for her invaluable help with this project. Thanks go out to Nancy Britt for her excellent editing work. Also to be thanked are Dr. Kennedy's secretaries, Mary Anne Bunker and Ruth Rohm. Additional thanks to John Aman, and Norm Wise and Linda Root, who worked on the earlier version of this book.

Appendix

350 Prophecies Fulfilled in Jesus Christ

The following is a list of 350 prophecies, many of which we have already examined in depth throughout this book. This list comes courtesy of According to the Scriptures in Manitoba, Canada (www.AccordingtotheScriptures.org).

Prophecy		Fulfillment
1. Genesis 3:15	Seed of a woman (virgin birth)	Galatians 4:4-5, Matthew 1:18
2. Genesis 3:15	He will bruise Satan's Head	Hebrews 2:14, 1 John 3:18
3. Genesis 5:24	The bodily ascension to heaven illustrated	Mark 16:19
4. Genesis 9:26, 27	The God of Shem will be the Son of Shem	Luke 3:36
5. Genesis 12:3	Seed of Abraham will bless all nations	Galatians 3:8, Acts 3:25, 26
6. Genesis 12:7	The Promise made to Abraham's Seed	Galatians 3:16
7. Genesis 14:18	A priest after the order of Melchizedek	Hebrews 6:20
8. Genesis 14:18	King of Peace and Righteousness	Hebrews 7:2
9. Genesis 14:18	The Last Supper foreshadowed	Matthew 26:26-29
10. Genesis 17:19	Seed of Isaac (Genesis 21:12)	Romans 9:7
11. Genesis 22:8	The Lamb of God promised	John 1:29
12. Genesis 22:18	As Isaac's seed, will bless all nations	Galatians 3:16
13. Genesis 26:2-5	The Seed of Isaac promised as the Redeemer	Hebrews 11:18
14. Genesis 28:12	The Bridge to heaven	John 1:51
15. Genesis 28:14	The Seed of Jacob	Luke 3:34
16. Genesis 49:10	The time of His coming	Luke 2:1-7; Galatians 4:4
17. Genesis 49:10	The Seed of Judah	Luke 3:33
18. Genesis 49:10	Called Shiloh or One Sent	John 17:3
19. Genesis 49:10	Messiah to come before Judah lost identity	John 11:47-52
20. Genesis 49:10	Unto Him shall the obedience of the people be	John 10:16
21. Exodus 3:13-15	The Great "I AM"	John 4:26, 8:58
22. Exodus 12:5	A Lamb without blemish	Hebrews 9:14; 1 Peter 1:19
23. Exodus 12:13	The blood of the Lamb saves from wrath	Romans 5:8
24. Exodus 12:21-27	Christ is our Passover	1 Corinthians 5:7
25. Exodus 12:46	Not a bone of the Lamb to be broken	John 19:31-36
26. Exodus 15:2	His exaltation predicted as Yeshua	Acts 7:55, 56
27. Exodus 15:11	His Character—Holiness	Luke 1:35; Acts 4:27
28. Exodus 17:6	The Spiritual Rock of Israel	1 Corinthians 10:4
29. Exodus 33:19	His Character—Merciful	Luke 1:72
30. Leviticus 1:2-9	His sacrifice a sweet smelling savor unto God	Ephesians 5:2
31. Leviticus 14:11	The leper cleansed—Sign to priesthood	Luke 5:12-14; Acts 6:7
32. Leviticus 16:15-17	Prefigures Christ's once-for-all death	Hebrews 9:7-14
33. Leviticus 16:27	Suffering outside the camp	Matthew 27:33; Heb. 13:11, 12
34. Leviticus 17:11	The Blood—the life of the flesh	Matthew 26:28; Mark 10:45
35. Leviticus 17:11	It is the blood that makes atonement	Romans 3:23-24; 1 John 1:7
36. Leviticus 23:36-37	The Drink-offering: "If any man thirst"	John 7:37
37. Numbers 9:12	Not a bone of Him broken	John 19:31-36
38. Numbers 21:9	The serpent on a pole—Christ lifted up	John 3:14-18, 12:32

39. Numbers 24:17	Time: "I shall see him, but not now."	John 1:14; Galatians 4:4
40. Deuteronomy 18:15	"This is of a truth that prophet."	John 6:14
41. Deuteronomy 18:15-16	"Had ye believed Moses, ye would believe me."	John 5:45-47
42. Deuteronomy 18:18	Sent by the Father to speak His word	John 8:28, 29
43. Deuteronomy 18:19	Whoever will not hear must bear his sin	Acts 3:22-23
44. Deuteronomy 21:23	Cursed is He that hangs on a tree	Galatians 3:10-13
45. Joshua 5:14-15	The Captain of our salvation	Hebrews 2:10
46. Ruth 4:4-10	Christ, our kinsman, has redeemed us	Ephesians 1:3-7
47. 1 Samuel 2:10	Shall be an anointed King to the Lord	Matthew 28:18, John 12:15
48. 2 Samuel 7:12	David's Seed	Matthew 1:1
49. 2 Samuel 7:13	His Kingdom is everlasting	2 Peter 1:11
50. 2 Samuel 7:14a	The Son of God	Luke 1:32, Romans 1:3-4
51. 2 Samuel 7:16	David's house established forever	Luke 3:31; Revelation 22:16
52. 2 Kings 2:11	The bodily ascension to heaven illustrated	Luke 24:51
53. 1 Chronicles 17:11	David's Seed	Matthew 1:1, 9:27
54. 1 Chronicles 17:12-13	To reign on David's throne forever	Luke 1:32, 33
55. 1 Chronicles 17:13	"I will be His Father, He ... my Son."	Hebrews 1:5
56. Job 9:32-33	Mediator between man and God	1 Timothy 2:5
57. Job 19:23-27	The Resurrection predicted	John 5:24-29
58. Psalm 2:1-3	The enmity of kings foreordained	Acts 4:25-28
59. Psalm 2:2	To own the title, Anointed (Christ)	John 1:41, Acts 2:36
60. Psalm 2:6	His Character—Holiness	John 8:46; Revelation 3:7
61. Psalm 2:6	To own the title King	Matthew 2:2
62. Psalm 2:7	Declared the Beloved Son	Matthew 3:17, Romans 1:4
63. Psalm 2:7, 8	The Crucifixion and Resurrection intimated	Acts 13:29-33
64. Psalm 2:8, 9	Rule the nations with a rod of iron	Revelation 2:27, 12:5, 19:15
65. Psalm 2:12	Life comes through faith in Him	John 20:31
66. Psalm 8:2	The mouths of babes perfect His praise	Matthew 21:16
67. Psalm 8:5, 6	His humiliation and exaltation	Hebrews 2:5-9
68. Psalm 9:7-10	Judge the world in righteousness	Acts 17:31
69. Psalm 16:10	Was not to see corruption	Acts 2:31, 13:35
70. Psalm 16:9-11	Was to arise from the dead	John 20:9
71. Psalm 17:15	The resurrection predicted	Luke 24:6
72. Psalm 18:2-3	The horn of salvation	Luke 1:69-71
73. Psalm 22:1	Forsaken because of sins of others	2 Corinthians 5:21
74. Psalm 22:1	"My God, my God, why hast thou forsaken me?"	Matthew 27:46
75. Psalm 22:2	Darkness upon Calvary for three hours	Matthew 27:45
76. Psalm 22:7	They shoot out the lip and shake the Head	Matthew 27:39-44
77. Psalm 22:8	"He trusted in God, let Him deliver Him"	Matthew 27:43
78. Psalm 22:9-10	Born the Saviour	Luke 2:7
79. Psalm 22:12-13	They seek His death	John 19:6
80. Psalm 22:14	His blood poured out when they pierced His side	John 19:34
81. Psalm 22:14-15	Suffered agony on Calvary	Mark 15:34-37
82. Psalm 22:15	He thirsted	John 19:28
83. Psalm 22:16	They pierced His hands and His feet	John 19:34, 37; 20:27
84. Psalm 22:17-18	Stripped Him before the stares of men	Luke 23:34-35
85. Psalm 22:18	They parted His garments	John 19:23-24
86. Psalm 22:20-21	He committed Himself to God	Luke 23:46
87. Psalm 22:20-21	Satanic power bruising the Redeemer's Heel	Hebrews 2:14
88. Psalm 22:22	His Resurrection declared	John 20:17
89. Psalm 22:27-28	He shall be the governor of the nations	Colossians 1:16
90. Psalm 22:31	"It is finished"	John 19:30, Hebrews 10:10, 12, 14, 18
91. Psalm 23:1	"I am the Good Shepherd"	John 10:11, 1 Peter 2:25

92. Psalm 24:3	His exaltation predicted	Acts 1:11, Philippians 2:9
93. Psalm 30:3	His resurrection predicted	Acts 2:32
94. Psalm 31:5	"Into thy hands I commit my spirit"	Luke 23:46
95. Psalm 31:11	His acquaintances fled from Him	Mark 14:50
96. Psalm 31:13	They took counsel to put Him to death	Matthew 27:1, John 11:53
97. Psalm 31:14-15	"He trusted in God, let Him deliver him"	Matthew 27:43
98. Psalm 34:20	Not a bone of Him broken	John 19:31-36
99. Psalm 35:11	False witnesses rose up against Him	Matthew 26:59
100. Psalm 35:19	He was hated without a cause	John 15:25
101. Psalm 38:11	His friends stood afar off	Luke 23:49
102. Psalm 38:12	Enemies try to entangle Him by craft	Mark 14:1, Matthew 22:15
103. Psalm 38:12-13	Silent before His accusers	Matthew 27:12-14
104. Psalm 38:20	He went about doing good	Acts 10:38
105. Psalm 40:2-5	The joy of His resurrection predicted	John 20:20
106. Psalm 40:6-8	His delight—the will of the Father	John 4:34, Hebrews 10:5-10
107. Psalm 40:9	He was to preach the Righteousness in Israel	Matthew 4:17
108. Psalm 40:14	Confronted by adversaries in the Garden	John 18:4-6
109. Psalm 41:9	Betrayed by a familiar friend	John 13:18
110. Psalm 45:2	Words of Grace come from His lips	John 1:17, Luke 4:22
111. Psalm 45:6	To own the title, God or Elohim	Hebrews 1:8
112. Psalm 45:7	A special anointing by the Holy Spirit	Matthew 3:16; Hebrews 1:9
113. Psalm 45:7-8	Called the Christ (Messiah or Anointed)	Luke 2:11
114. Psalm 45:17	His name remembered forever	Ephesians 1:20-21, Hebrews 1:8
115. Psalm 55:12-14	Betrayed by a friend, not an enemy	John 13:18
116. Psalm 55:15	Unrepentant death of the Betrayer	Matthew 27:3-5, Acts 1:16-19
117. Psalm 68:18	To give gifts to men	Ephesians 4:7-16
118. Psalm 68:18	Ascended into heaven	Luke 24:51
119. Psalm 69:4	Hated without a cause	John 15:25
120. Psalm 69:8	A stranger to own brethren	John 1:11, 7:5
121. Psalm 69:9	Zealous for the Lord's House	John 2:17
122. Psalm 69:14-20	Messiah's anguish of soul before crucifixion	Matthew 26:36-45
123. Psalm 69:20	"My soul is exceeding sorrowful."	Matthew 26:38
124. Psalm 69:21	Given vinegar in thirst	Matthew 27:34
125. Psalm 69:26	The Saviour given and smitten by God	John 17:4, 18:11
126. Psalm 72:10-11	Great persons were to visit Him	Matthew 2:1-11
127. Psalm 72:16	The corn of wheat to fall into the Ground	John 12:24-25
128. Psalm 72:17	Belief on His name will produce offspring	John 1:12-13
129. Psalm 72:17	All nations shall be blessed by Him	Galatians 3:8
130. Psalm 72:17	All nations shall call Him blessed	John 12:13, Revelation 5:8-12
131. Psalm 78:1-2	He would teach in parables	Matthew 13:34-35
132. Psalm 78:2b	To speak the Wisdom of God with authority	Matthew 7:29
133. Psalm 80:17	The Man of God's right hand	Mark 14:61-62
134. Psalm 88	The Suffering and Reproach of Calvary	Matthew 27:26-50
135. Psalm 88:8	They stood afar off and watched	Luke 23:49
136. Psalm 89:27	Firstborn	Colossians 1:15, 18
137. Psalm 89:27	Emmanuel to be higher than earthly kings	Luke 1:32-33
138. Psalm 89:35-37	David's Seed, throne, kingdom endure forever	Luke 1:32-33
139. Psalm 89:36-37	His character—Faithfulness	Revelation 1:5, 19:11
140. Psalm 90:2	He is from everlasting (Micah 5:2)	John 1:1
141. Psalm 91:11-12	Identified as Messianic; used to tempt Christ	Luke 4:10-11
142. Psalm 97:9	His exaltation predicted	Acts 1:11, Ephesians 1:20
143. Psalm 100:5	His character—Goodness	Matthew 19:16-17
144. Psalm 102:1-11	The Suffering and Reproach of Calvary	John 19:16-30
145. Psalm 102:25-27	Messiah is the Preexistent Son	Hebrews 1:10-12

146. Psalm 109:25	Ridiculed	Matthew 27:39
147. Psalm 110:1	Son of David	Matthew 22:42-43
148. Psalm 110:1	To ascend to the right hand of the Father	Mark 16:19
149. Psalm 110:1	David's Son called Lord	Matthew 22:44-45
150. Psalm 110:4	A priest after Melchizedek's order	Hebrews 6:20
151. Psalm 112:4	His character—Compassionate, Gracious, et al	Matthew 9:36
152. Psalm 118:17-18	Messiah's Resurrection assured	Luke 24:5-7; 1 Corinthians 15:20
153. Psalm 118:22-23	The rejected stone is Head of the corner	Matthew 21:42-43
154. Psalm 118:26a	The Blessed One presented to Israel	Matthew 21:9
155. Psalm 118:26b	To come while temple standing	Matthew 21:12-15
156. Psalm 132:11	The Seed of David (the fruit of His Body)	Luke 1:32, Acts 2:30
157. Psalm 129:3	He was scourged	Matthew 27:26
158. Psalm 138:1-6	The supremacy of David's Seed amazes kings	Matthew 2:2-6
159. Psalm 147:3, 6	The earthly ministry of Christ described	Luke 4:18
160. Proverbs 1:23	He will send the Spirit of God	John 16:7
161. Proverbs 8:23	Foreordained from everlasting	Revelation 13:8, 1 Peter 1:19-20
162. Song of Solomon 5:16	The altogether lovely One	John 1:17
163. Isaiah 2:3	He shall teach all nations	John 4:25
164. Isaiah 2:4	He shall judge among the nations	John 5:22
165. Isaiah 6:1	When Isaiah saw His glory	John 12:40-41
166. Isaiah 6:8	The One Sent by God	John 12:38-45
167. Isaiah 6:9-10	Parables fall on deaf ears	Matthew 13:13-15
168. Isaiah 6:9-12	Blinded to Christ and deaf to His words	Acts 28:23-29
169. Isaiah 7:14	To be born of a virgin	Luke 1:35
170. Isaiah 7:14	To be Emmanuel—God with us	Matthew 1:18-23, 1 Timothy 3:16
171. Isaiah 8:8	Called Emmanuel	Matthew 28:20
172. Isaiah 8:14	A stone of stumbling, a Rock of offense	1 Peter 2:8
173. Isaiah 9:1, 2	His ministry to begin in Galilee	Matthew 4:12-17
174. Isaiah 9:6	A child born—Humanity	Luke 1:31
175. Isaiah 9:6	A Son given—Deity	Luke 1:32, John 1:14, 1 Timothy 3:16
176. Isaiah 9:6	Declared to be the Son of God with power	Romans 1:3-4
177. Isaiah 9:6	The Wonderful One, Peleh	Luke 4:22
178. Isaiah 9:6	The Counsellor, Yaatz	Matthew 13:54
179. Isaiah 9:6	The Mighty God, El Gibor	1 Corinthians 1:24, Titus 2:3
180. Isaiah 9:6	The Everlasting Father, Avi Adth	John 8:58, 10:30
181. Isaiah 9:6	The Prince of Peace, Sar Shalom	John 16:33
182. Isaiah 9:7	To establish an everlasting kingdom	Luke 1:32-33
183. Isaiah 9:7	His Character—Just	John 5:30
184. Isaiah 9:7	No end to his Government, Throne, and Peace	Luke 1:32-33
185. Isaiah 11:1	Called a Nazarene—the Branch, Netzer	Matthew 2:23
186. Isaiah 11:1	A rod out of Jesse—Son of Jesse	Luke 3:23, 32
187. Isaiah 11:2	Anointed One by the Spirit	Matthew 3:16-17, Acts 10:38
188. Isaiah 11:2	His Character—Wisdom, Knowledge, et al.	Colossians 2:3
189. Isaiah 11:3	He would know their thoughts	Luke 6:8, John 2:25
190. Isaiah 11:4	Judge in righteousness	Acts 17:31
191. Isaiah 11:4	Judges with the sword of His mouth	Revelation 2:16; 19:11,15
192. Isaiah 11:5	His Character—Righteous & Faithful	Revelation 19:11
193. Isaiah 11:10	The Gentiles seek Him	John 12:18-21
194. Isaiah 12:2	Called Jesus—Yeshua	Matthew 1:21
195. Isaiah 22:22	The One given all authority to govern	Revelation 3:7
196. Isaiah 25:8	The Resurrection predicted	1 Corinthians 15:54
197. Isaiah 26:19	His power of Resurrection predicted	Matthew 27:50-54
198. Isaiah 28:16	The Messiah is the precious cornerstone	Acts 4:11-12

199. Isaiah 28:16	The Sure Foundation	1 Corinthians 3:11, Matthew 16:18
200. Isaiah 29:13	He indicated hypocritical obedience to His Word	Matthew 15:7-9
201. Isaiah 29:14	The wise are confounded by the Word	1 Corinthians 1:18-31
202. Isaiah 32:2	A Refuge—A man shall be a hiding place	Matthew 23:37
203. Isaiah 35:4	He will come and save you	Matthew 1:21
204. Isaiah 35:5-6	To have a ministry of miracles	Matthew 11:2-6
205. Isaiah 40:3-4	Preceded by forerunner	John 1:23
206. Isaiah 40:9	"Behold your God."	John 1:36, 19:14
207. Isaiah 40:10	He will come to reward	Revelation 22:12
208. Isaiah 40:11	A shepherd—compassionate life-giver	John 10:10-18
209. Isaiah 42:1-4	The Servant—as a faithful, patient redeemer	Matthew 12:18-21
210. Isaiah 42:2	Meek and lowly	Matthew 11:28-30
211. Isaiah 42:3	He brings hope for the hopeless	John 4
212. Isaiah 42:4	The nations shall wait on His teachings	John 12:20-26
213. Isaiah 42:6	The Light (salvation) of the Gentiles	Luke 2:32
214. Isaiah 42:1, 6	His is a worldwide compassion	Matthew 28:19-20
215. Isaiah 42:7	Blind eyes opened	John 9:25-38
216. Isaiah 43:11	He is the only Saviour	Acts 4:12
217. Isaiah 44:3	He will send the Spirit of God	John 16:7, 13
218. Isaiah 45:21-25	He is Lord and Saviour	Philippians 3:20, Titus 2:13
219. Isaiah 45:23	He will be the Judge	John 5:22, Romans 14:11
220. Isaiah 46:9-10	Declares things not yet done	John 13:19
221. Isaiah 48:12	The First and the Last	John 1:30; Revelation 1:8, 17
222. Isaiah 48:16-17	He came as a Teacher	John 3:2
223. Isaiah 49:1	Called from the womb—His humanity	Matthew 1:18
224. Isaiah 49:5	A Servant from the womb	Luke 1:31, Philippians 2:7
225. Isaiah 49:6	He will restore Israel	Acts 3:19-21, 15:16-17
226. Isaiah 49:6	He is Salvation for Israel	Luke 2:29-32
227. Isaiah 49:6	He is the Light of the Gentiles	John 8:12, Acts 13:47
228. Isaiah 49:6	He is Salvation unto the ends of the earth	Acts 15:7-18
229. Isaiah 49:7	He is despised of the Nation	John 1:11, 8:48-49, 19:14-15
230. Isaiah 50:3	Heaven is clothed in black at His humiliation	Luke 23:44-45
231. Isaiah 50:4	He is a learned counselor for the weary	Matthew 7:29, 11:28-29
232. Isaiah 50:5	The Servant bound willingly to obedience	Matthew 26:39
233. Isaiah 50:6a	"I gave my back to the smiters."	Matthew 27:26
234. Isaiah 50:6b	He was smitten on the cheeks	Matthew 26:67
235. Isaiah 50:6c	He was spat upon	Matthew 27:30
236. Isaiah 52:7	Published good tidings upon mountains	Matthew 5:12, 15:29, 28:16
237. Isaiah 52:13	The Servant exalted Acts 1:8-11, Ephesians 1:19-22, Philippians 2:5-9
238. Isaiah 52:14	The Servant shockingly abused Luke 18:31-34, Matthew 26:67-68
239. Isaiah 52:15	Nations startled by message of the Servant	Luke 18:31-34, Matthew 26:67-68
240. Isaiah 52:15	His blood shed sprinkles nations	Hebrews 9:13-14, Revelation 1:5
241. Isaiah 53:1	His people would not believe Him	John 12:37-38
242. Isaiah 53:2	Appearance of an ordinary man	Philippians 2:6-8
243. Isaiah 53:3a	Despised	Luke 4:28-29
244. Isaiah 53:3b	Rejected	Matthew 27:21-23
245. Isaiah 53:3c	Great sorrow and grief Matthew 26:37-38, Luke 19:41, Hebrews 4:15
246. Isaiah 53:3d	Men hide from being associated with Him	Mark 14:50-52
247. Isaiah 53:4a	He would have a Healing ministry	Matthew 8:16-17
248. Isaiah 53:4b	Thought to be cursed by God	Matthew 26:66, 27:41-43
249. Isaiah 53:5a	Bears penalty for mankind's iniquities	2 Corinthians 5:21, Hebrews 2:9
250. Isaiah 53:5b	His sacrifice provides peace between man and God	Colossians 1:20
251. Isaiah 53:5c	His sacrifice would Heal man of sin	1 Peter 2:24

252. Isaiah 53:6a	He would be the sin-bearer for all mankind	1 John 2:2, 4:10
253. Isaiah 53:6b	God's will that He bear sin for all mankind	Galatians 1:4
254. Isaiah 53:7a	Oppressed and afflicted	Matthew 27:27-31
255. Isaiah 53:7b	Silent before his accusers	Matthew 27:12-14
256. Isaiah 53:7c	Sacrificial lamb	John 1:29, 1 Peter 1:18-19
257. Isaiah 53:8a	Confined and persecuted	Matthew 26:47-27:31
258. Isaiah 53:8b	He would be judged	John 18:13-22
259. Isaiah 53:8c	Killed	Matthew 27:35
260. Isaiah 53:8d	Dies for the sins of the world	1 John 2:2
261. Isaiah 53:9a	Buried in a rich man's grave	Matthew 27:57
262. Isaiah 53:9b	Innocent and had done no violence	Luke 23:41, John 18:38
263. Isaiah 53:9c	No deceit in his mouth	1 Peter 2:22
264. Isaiah 53:10a	God's will that He die for mankind	John 18:11
265. Isaiah 53:10b	An offering for sin	Matthew 20:28, Galatians 3:13
266. Isaiah 53:10c	Resurrected and live forever	Romans 6:9
267. Isaiah 53:10d	He would prosper	John 17:1-5
268. Isaiah 53:11a	God fully satisfied with His suffering	John 12:27
269. Isaiah 53:11b	God's servant would justify man	Romans 5:8-9, 18-19
270. Isaiah 53:11c	The sin-bearer for all mankind	Hebrews 9:28
271. Isaiah 53:12a	Exalted by God because of his sacrifice	Matthew 28:18
272. Isaiah 53:12b	He would give up his life to save mankind	Luke 23:46
273. Isaiah 53:12c	Numbered with the transgressors	Mark 15:27-28
274. Isaiah 53:12d	Sin-bearer for all mankind	1 Peter 2:24
275. Isaiah 53:12e	Intercede to God in behalf of mankind	Luke 23:34, Romans 8:34
276. Isaiah 55:3	Resurrected by God	Acts 13:34
277. Isaiah 55:4a	A witness	John 18:37
278. Isaiah 55:4b	He is a leader and commander	Hebrews 2:10
279. Isaiah 55:5	God would glorify Him	Acts 3:13
280. Isaiah 59:16a	Intercessor between man and God	Matthew 10:32
281. Isaiah 59:16b	He would come to provide salvation	John 6:40
282. Isaiah 59:20	He would come to Zion as their Redeemer	Luke 2:38
283. Isaiah 60:1-3	He would shew light to the Gentiles	Acts 26:23
284. Isaiah 61:1a	The Spirit of God upon him	Matthew 3:16-17
285. Isaiah 61:1b	The Messiah would preach the good news	Luke 4:16-21
286. Isaiah 61:1c	Provide freedom from the bondage of sin	John 8:31-36
287. Isaiah 61:1-2a	Proclaim a period of grace	Galatians 4:4-5
288. Jeremiah 23:5-6	Descendant of David	Luke 3:23-31
289. Jeremiah 23:5-6	The Messiah would be both God and Man	John 13:13, 1 Timothy 3:16
290. Jeremiah 31:22	Born of a virgin	Matthew 1:18-20
291. Jeremiah 31:31	The Messiah would be the new covenant	Matthew 26:28
292. Jeremiah 33:14-15	Descendant of David	Luke 3:23-31
293. Ezekiel 34:23-24	Descendant of David	Matthew 1:1
294. Ezekiel 37:24-25	Descendant of David	Luke 1:31-33
295. Daniel 2:44-45	The Stone that shall break the kingdoms	Matthew 21:44
296. Daniel 7:13-14a	He would ascend into heaven	Acts 1:9-11
297. Daniel 7:13-14b	Highly exalted	Ephesians 1:20-22
298. Daniel 7:13-14c	His dominion would be everlasting	Luke 1:31-33
299. Daniel 9:24a	To make an end to sins	Galatians 1:3-5
300. Daniel 9:24a	To make reconciliation for iniquity	Romans 5:10, 2 Corinthians 5:18-21
301. Daniel 9:24b	He would be holy	Luke 1:35
302. Daniel 9:25	His announcement	John 12:12-13
303. Daniel 9:26a	Cut off	Matthew 16:21, 21:38-39
304. Daniel 9:26b	Die for the sins of the world	Hebrews 2:9
305. Daniel 9:26c	Killed before the destruction of the temple	Matthew 27:50-51

306. Daniel 10:5-6	Messiah in a glorified state	Revelation 1:13-16
307. Hosea 11:1	He would be called out of Egypt	Matthew 2:15
308. Hosea 13:14	He would defeat death	1 Corinthians 15:55-57
309. Joel 2:32	Offer salvation to all mankind	Romans 10:9-13
310. Jonah 1:17	Death and resurrection of Christ	Matthew 12:40, 16:4
311. Micah 5:2a	Born in Bethlehem	Matthew 2:1-6
312. Micah 5:2b	Ruler in Israel	Luke 1:33
313. Micah 5:2c	From everlasting	John 8:58
314. Haggai 2:6-9	He would visit the second temple	Luke 2:27-32
315. Haggai 2:23	Descendant of Zerubbabel	Luke 2:27-32
316. Zechariah 3:8	God's servant	John 17:4
317. Zechariah 6:12-13	Priest and King	Hebrews 8:1
318. Zechariah 9:9a	Greeted with rejoicing in Jerusalem	Matthew 21:8-10
319. Zechariah 9:9b	Beheld as King	John 12:12-13
320. Zechariah 9:9c	The Messiah would be just	John 5:30
321. Zechariah 9:9d	The Messiah would bring salvation	Luke 19:10
322. Zechariah 9:9e	The Messiah would be humble	Matthew 11:29
323. Zechariah 9:9f	Presented to Jerusalem riding on a donkey	Matthew 21:6-9
324. Zechariah 10:4	The cornerstone	Ephesians 2:20
325. Zechariah 11:4-6a	At His coming, Israel to have unfit leaders	Matthew 23:1-4
326. Zechariah 11:4-6b	Rejection causes God to remove His protection	Luke 19:41-44
327. Zechariah 11:4-6c	Rejected in favor of another king	John 19:13-15
328. Zechariah 11:7	Ministry to "poor," the believing remnant	Matthew 9:35-36
329. Zechariah 11:8a	Unbelief forces Messiah to reject them	Matthew 23:33
330. Zechariah 11:8b	Despised	Matthew 27:20
331. Zechariah 11:9	Stops ministering to those who rejected Him	Matthew 13:10-11
332. Zechariah 11:10-11a	Rejection causes God to remove protection	Luke 19:41-44
333. Zechariah 11:10-11b	The Messiah would be God	John 14:7
334. Zechariah 11:12-13a	Betrayed for thirty pieces of silver	Matthew 26:14-15
335. Zechariah 11:12-13b	Rejected	Matthew 26:14-15
336. Zechariah 11:12-13c	Thirty pieces of silver cast in the house of the Lord	Matthew 27:3-5
337. Zechariah 11:12-13d	The Messiah would be God	John 12:45
338. Zechariah 12:10a	The Messiah's body would be pierced	John 19:34-37
339. Zechariah 12:10b	The Messiah would be both God and man	John 10:30
340. Zechariah 12:10c	The Messiah would be rejected	John 1:11
341. Zechariah 13:7a	God's will He die for mankind	John 18:11
342. Zechariah 13:7b	A violent death	Mark 14:27
343. Zechariah 13:7c	Both God and man	John 14:9
344. Zechariah 13:7d	Israel scattered as a result of rejecting Him	Matthew 26:31-56
345. Zechariah 14:4	He would return to the Mount of Olives	Acts 1:11-12
346. Malachi 3:1a	Messenger to prepare the way for Messiah	Mark 1:1-8
347. Malachi 3:1b	Sudden appearance at the temple	Mark 11:15-16
348. Malachi 3:1c	Messenger of the new covenant	Luke 4:43
349. Malachi 4:5	Forerunner in spirit of Elijah	Matthew 3:1-3, 11:10-14, 17:11-13
350. Malachi 4:6	Forerunner would turn many to righteousness	Luke 1:16-17

Endnotes

1   Jesus finished the job in the sense that He accomplished as the Second Adam what the first Adam failed to do (Romans 5:14).

2   D. James Kennedy, *The Real Meaning of the Zodiac* (Ft. Lauderdale: Coral Ridge Ministries, 1989).

3   Transcript of an interview with Rabbi Moshe Laurie, conducted by Jerry Newcombe on location in Connecticut (Ft. Lauderdale: Coral Ridge Ministries-TV, November 2004).

4   In Matthew's gospel, we see an exception to that rule. We see the gospel of grace already at work where some women with sinful pasts (e.g., Bathsheba) were nonetheless in the lineage of the Savior.

5   Dr. Donald Grey Barnhouse, Christmas card, Philadelphia, 1956.

6   See "Nostradamus Predicted the Terrorist Attack on New York-Fiction!" at http://www.truthorfiction.com/rumors/t/terrorpredict.htm

7   Walter A. Elwell, *Encyclopedia Of The Bible* (Grand Rapids, Mich.: Zondervan Publishing House, 1973) 1446-7.

8   Adrian Rogers, *Revelation: Volume 2* (Memphis, TN: Love Worth Finding, 1995) 9.

9   James C. Hefley, *What's So Great About the Bible* (Elgin, IL: David C. Cook, 1969) 24-5.

10 Interview with Lee Strobel in D. James Kennedy, *The Bible: Fable, Fraud or Fact?* (Ft. Lauderdale: Coral Ridge Ministries-TV, 1994).

11 Lee Strobel, *Inside the Mind of Unchurched Harry & Mary: How to Reach Friends and Family Who Avoid God and the Church* (Grand Rapids, Mich.: Zondervan Publishing House, 1973) 36.

12 Peter Stoner, *Science Speaks* (Chicago: Moody Press, 1963) 109. Quoted in Josh McDowell, *Evidence That Demands a Verdict* (San Bernardino, Calif.: Campus Crusade for Christ, 1972) 167.

13 Lee Strobel, *Inside the Mind of Unchurched Harry & Mary: How to Reach Friends and Family Who Avoid God and the Church* (Grand Rapids, Mich.: Zondervan Publishing House, 1973) 37.

14 Ibid.

15 Ibid.

16 Herbert Lockyer, *All the Messianic Prophecies of the Bible* (Grand Rapids, Mich.: Zondervan Publishing House, 1973) 58.

17 Transcript of an interview of Dr. Amy-Jill Levine, conducted by Jerry Newcombe on location at Vanderbilt Divinity School in Nashville (Ft. Lauderdale: Coral Ridge Ministries-TV, 2000).

18 Ibid.

19 Ibid.

20 Transcript of an interview of Dr. Edwin Yamauchi, conducted by Jerry Newcombe on location at the University of Miami (Ohio) (Ft. Lauderdale: Coral Ridge Ministries-TV, 2000).

21 Hugh J. Schonfield, *The Passover Plot: A New Interpretation of the Life and Death of Jesus* (Shaftesbury, Dorset, et al: Element, 1965 / 1996) 53.

22 Ibid., 139.

23 Ibid., 307.
24 Ibid., 194.
25 Ibid., 196.
26 Ibid., 206.
27 Ibid.
28 Principal Hill, *Lectures in Divinity*, Vol. I, pp. 47-8. Quoted in William Taylor, *The Miracles of Our Saviour* (New York: Hodder and Stoughton, 1890) 21-22.
29 Transcript of an interview of Dr. Samuel Lamerson, conducted by Jerry Newcombe on location at Knox Theological Seminary in Ft. Lauderdale (Ft. Lauderdale: Coral Ridge Ministries-TV, 2000).
30 Ibid.
31 Ibid.
32 Transcript of an interview of Dr. Paul L. Maier, conducted by Jerry Newcombe on location at Western Michigan University in Kalamazoo (Ft. Lauderdale: Coral Ridge Ministries-TV, 2000).
33 Transcript of an interview of Dr. Paul Feinberg, conducted by Jerry Newcombe on location at Trinity Evangelical Divinity School in Deerfield, Illinois (Ft. Lauderdale: Coral Ridge Ministries-TV, 2000).
34 Transcript of an interview with Dr. Samuel Lamerson.
35 Transcript of an interview with Dr. Edwin Yamauchi.
36 Transcript of an interview of Dr. N. T. Wright, conducted by Jerry Newcombe on location at Westminster Abbey in London (Ft. Lauderdale: Coral Ridge Ministries-TV, 2000).
37 Ibid.
38 Ibid.
39 Ibid.
40 Ibid.
41 Transcript of an interview of Father Francis Martin, conducted by Jerry Newcombe on location near Washington, D. C. (Ft. Lauderdale: Coral Ridge Ministries-TV, 2000).
42 For detail after detail on these points, please see D. James Kennedy and Jerry Newcombe, *What If Jesus Had Never Been Born?* (Nashville: Thomas Nelson, 1994) and *What If the Bible Had Never Been Written?* (Nashville: Thomas Nelson, 1998).
43 Dr. F. J. Meldau in Herbert Lockyer, *All The Messianic Prophecies of the Bible* (Grand Rapids, Mich.: Zondervan Publishing House, 1973) 63.
44 Transcript of an interview of Dr. Samuel Lamerson, conducted by Jerry Newcombe on location at Knox Theological Seminary in Ft. Lauderdale (Ft. Lauderdale: Coral Ridge Ministries-TV, 2000).
45 Matthew Henry, *Commentary on the Whole Bible: New One Volume Edition* (Grand Rapids, Mich.: Zondervan Publishing House, 1973) 840.
46 Faculty of Theology of the University of Navarre, *The Navarre Bible: Saint Luke's Gospel* (Dublin: Four Courts Press, 1991) 59.
47 Max Lucado, *The Applause of Heaven* (Dallas: Word Publishing, 1995) 8.
48 Matthew Henry, *Commentary on the Whole Bible,* Isaiah XXXV, http://www.ccel.org/ccel/henry/mhc4.Is.xxxvi.html
49 Ibid.

50 Transcript of an interview with Mike Licona, conducted by Jerry Newcombe, on location at Virginia Beach (Fort Lauderdale: Coral Ridge Ministries-TV, 2004).

51 Paul L. Maier, *In The Fullness of Time* (Grand Rapids, Mich.: Kregel Publi-
cations, 1997) 99-100.

52 If you would like more information to help you get grounded in the
Christian faith, write to Coral Ridge Ministries, Box 40, Ft. Lauderdale,
FL 33308 and ask for *Beginning Again.* You may also make your request
when you call 1-800-988-7884 or visit www.coralridge.org. Co-author
Jerry Newcombe highly recommends a book that has helped him. It is a
three-year through-the-Bible study guide, *Search the Scriptures*, edited by
Alan Stibbs (Downers Grove, Ill.: InterVarsity Press, 1949, 1974). It's now
out in paperback.

Index